Spiritual Reflections
on the Sunday Gospels, **Cycle C**

To
Praise,
To
Bless,
To
Preach

Peter John Cameron, O.P.

Our Sunday Visitor Publishing Division
Our Sunday Visitor, Inc.
Huntington, Indiana 46750

Nihil Obstat:

Francis J. McAree, S.T.D.
Censor Librorum

Imprimatur:

✠ Patrick J. Sheridan, D.D.
Vicar General, Archdiocese of New York
December 20, 1999

The majority of the Scripture citations in this work, whether vebatim or paraphrased, are from the *New American Bible With Revised New Testament,* copyright © 1986, 1970 by the Confraternity of Christian Doctrine, Inc., Washington, DC 20017. ALL RIGHTS RESERVED. Some verses are quoted from earlier versions. Excerpts from the *Lectionary for Mass for Use in the Dioceses of the United States of America, second typical edition* copyright © 1970, 1997, 1998 by the Confraternity of Christian Doctrine, Inc. ALL RIGHTS RESERVED. Excerpts from the English translation of the *Catechism of the Catholic Church* for use in the United States of America, copyright © 1994, United States Catholic Conference — Libreria Editrice Vaticana. Used with permission. If any copyrighted materials have been inadvertently used in this work without proper credit being given in one manner or another, please notify Our Sunday Visitor in writing so that future printings of this work may be corrected accordingly.

Our Sunday Visitor Publishing Division
Our Sunday Visitor, Inc.
200 Noll Plaza
Huntington, IN 46750

ISBN: 087973-823-5
LCCCN: 00-130351

Cover design by Rebecca Heaston
Edited by Lisa Grote
PRINTED IN THE UNITED STATES OF AMERICA

FOR MY NIECES AND NEPHEWS

MEGAN
JENNIFER
ZACHARY
JESSICA
ERIC
NICHOLAS
CAITLIN

WITH MY LOVE

TABLE OF CONTENTS

PART ONE: REFLECTIONS ON THE SUNDAY GOSPELS

PART TWO: REFLECTIONS ON SOLEMNITIES AND ALSO FEASTS THAT MAY FALL ON SUNDAY

PREFACE

One day a suspicious Cistercian who wasn't too certain about the genuineness of a new, unheard-of religious order sought a confirmatory sign. So he approached the altar, made the sign of the cross, and opened a Missal in the holy name of Jesus. At the top of the first page, containing a Preface of the Mass of Our Lady, he read, "To praise, to bless, and to preach." With that, his skepticism vanished and he commended himself to the prayers of the friars of the Order of Preachers — the Dominicans.

In an age filled with so much relativism, delusion, and doubt, we too look for some sign from heaven to keep us on the sure path to holiness and happiness. That assurance continues to come to us in the very same way: In the Word of God who is the Son of Mary. The more we reverently approach the Gospels with the name of Jesus on our lips and in our heart, the more does that living Word transform our life, dispelling all that threatens to deceive and discourage us. It is my prayer that these little meditations will aid in a personal renewal of the Gospel that magnifies the graces of the New Evangelization.

I am deeply thankful to Msgr. Francis McAree, the Rector of St. Joseph's Seminary-Dunwoodie, Sr. Regina Melican, O.P., Fr. Romanus Cessario, O.P., Fr. Greg Malovetz, David Burns, Lucille Kovary, and my seminary students for their generous support and assistance in the preparation of this volume.

Peter John Cameron, O.P.
July 22, 1999, Feast of St. Mary Magdalene
Patroness of the Order of Preachers

INTRODUCTION

WHY WE NEED THE NEW EVANGELIZATION

Pope John Paul II has lamented the way entire groups of the baptized have lost a living sense of the faith, and live a life far removed from Christ and his Gospel (*Redemptoris Missio,* 33). Elsewhere the Holy Father has spoken about "the crisis of civilization" that leaves people interiorly impoverished because of the tendency to forget God or to keep him at a distance (*Tertio Millennio Adveniente,* 52). In short, many people nowadays live under the curse of **distantiation**.

Distantiation refers to the plight of lives lived alienated from what truly matters, estranged from what we should love, disconnected from integrity, authenticity, and personal dignity, and cut off from the truth — the source of ultimate fulfillment. In effect, distantiation generates a state of "anti-creation" by reinstating the dark abyss that God set about to abolish when he created the earth (Gn 1:1-2). Sadly, unredeemed human nature prefers to dwell in this void. It favors the chasm and chaos to communion and sanctity.

To a great extent, even well-intentioned Christians can fall prey to the distantiating wiles of the world. But we can also bring distantiation upon ourselves through disillusioned notions and bad choices. In his encyclical *Fides et Ratio* (86-90), Pope John Paul II addresses five prevalent threats to orthodoxy, all of which distance us from God and his holy Church. *Eclecticism* is a form of relativism whereby one indiscriminately espouses certain attractive ideas in the world without due concern for any internal coherence. It debases wisdom to mere whim. Eclecticism impetuously disowns the very principles by which we can make sense of the "big picture." As a consequence, we end up knowing and defending only what we like. Eclecticism characterizes so-called "cafeteria Catholicism."

Historicism assumes an elitist way of looking at the past and of assessing the present. It denies the enduring primacy of Truth, and it sets up Purpose as a kind of demigod. In historicism, the only recognized rationality stems from what is relevant to the day. Historicism jettisons the precedents and prudence of former days, supplanting them for its

13

own self-styled, "better way" of judging things. Historicism leaves many important things up for grabs. Much of the dissent regarding the "big issues" in the Church gets fueled by historicism.

Scientism regards positive science as the only valid form of knowledge. Thus, to speak of "goods" or "values" is to lapse into the world of fantasy. Scientism vitiates values, reducing them to fictional constructs — the pathetic by-product of over-indulgent emotions and religiosity. Scientism lurks behind much of the "enlightened" world's disdain of the Christian faith and the Church's proclamation of the Mysteries.

Pragmatism advocates choice-making according to what is merely convenient or useful without due regard for ethical principles or divine Revelation. And *nihilism* preaches the negation of all objective truth. For the nihilist, freedom remains meaningless, our likeness to God imaginary, human dignity non-existent. How much pragmatism and nihilism drive pro-abortionists and all the other insidious denizens of the culture of death.

All of this must be countered by the Civilization of Love, mediated to a wounded and waiting world via the New Evangelization. Those at a distance must be drawn close to Jesus Christ, the heart of the New Evangelization.

THE HEART OF THE NEW EVANGELIZATION

To a certain extent, the need for a New Evangelization is the consequence of inadequate catechetics. In recent days, some catechetical ventures tend to downplay the truth that human persons are by nature religious, and therefore inherently spiritual. We cannot acquire a right regard for the Gospel unless we understand that we have been created in the image and likeness of God in Jesus Christ. Moreover, that image, disfigured by sin, needs to be restored to the divine image of God; only Jesus Christ can do this for us. We cannot do it on our own.

Yet, too often we minimize the centrality of Jesus Christ in salvation history and disparage his divinity as something distant and unreal. Cardinal Ratzinger has addressed this poignantly:

> We think that everyone knows about God already, that the
> subject of "God" has little to say to our everyday prob-

lems. Jesus corrects us: God is *the* practical, *the* realistic topic for man — in Jesus' time and in every time. As disciples of Jesus Christ, we have to give men what they most need — communion with the living God. Are we not all infected to varying degrees with an unacknowledged deism? We think that God is too far away, that he does not reach into our daily life; so, we say to ourselves, let's speak of close-at-hand, practical realities. No, says Jesus: God is present, he is within call. This is the first word of the Gospel, which changes our whole life when we put our faith in it. This has to be said to our world with completely new vigor on the authority of Christ. . . . Evangelization is the proclamation of God's nearness in word and deed together with instruction in his will through initiation into communion with Jesus Christ" (*Gospel, Catechesis, Catechism,* San Francisco: Ignatius Press, 1997, pp. 41, 63).

Thus, the heart of the New Evangelization is Jesus Christ himself. Pope John Paul II states it succinctly: "The vital core of the New Evangelization must be a clear and unequivocal proclamation of the person of Jesus Christ, that is, the preaching of his name, his teaching, his life, his promises, and the Kingdom that he has gained for us by his Paschal Mystery" (*Ecclesia in America,* 66).

In particular, the New Evangelization remains directed to the sanctification of culture in a way that illumines how Jesus Christ is part of — and transforms — every dimension of creation. To do this, the Holy Father emphasizes the need to inculturate preaching so that preachers proclaim the kerygma in the language and in the culture of its hearers.

What Is the New Evangelization?

If the heart of the New Evangelization is Jesus Christ who is the Good News (cf. Mk 1:1), then the task of the New Evangelization is to bring about **a renewal of the Gospel.** What is this Gospel that must be renewed? The *Catechism of the Catholic Church* (CCC) defines it this way: "The Gospel is the revelation in Jesus Christ of God's mercy to sinners" (1846). Dr. David

Schindler has commented that the primary need of our culture is for divine forgiveness, personal conversion, and a deepened sense of God's mercy. Only this liberation from the slavery of sin can accommodate our culture's desperate need for moral, social, and political reform.

ESSENTIAL PROPERTIES OF THE NEW EVANGELIZATION

Among the many properties of the New Evangelization, five outstanding ones should be considered. First of all, **the New Evangelization must be practical and appealing.** The proclamation of the Gospel must be as irresistible and appealing as Jesus Christ himself was to others when he walked the earth. This calls for tremendous creativity, ingenuity, innovation, and imagination. It begins in refusing to settle for tried-and-true, cliché, trivial, shallow, or pre-packaged presentations of the Gospel. It especially charges us to remain ever attentive to the goings-on of everyday life in order to find effective metaphors and analogies appropriate for translating the splendor of the Gospel in a compelling, satisfying manner.

Second, **the New Evangelization must proclaim Gospel morality.** The Gospel is not about validating worldly compromise, concession, or convenience. The Gospel is the revelation in Jesus Christ of God's mercy to sinners. Therefore, the New Evangelization must be realistic about the reality of sin, forceful in repudiating it, and masterful in enabling others to respond to the universal call to holiness. Obviously, only those devoted to sanctity can preach convincingly about the need for sanctity.

Third, **the New Evangelization must point to the true face of God and to the genuine meaning of human freedom.** Too many mistake freedom for unbridled license. Freedom is not autonomous, freestanding, or self-directed. Rather, authentic freedom exists only in an essential bond with truth and goodness. Freedom is truly free if it directs us to ultimate communion with God.

The gift of freedom is one of the outstanding manifestations of the divine image in us. God ordained to leave us in the power of our own counsel so that we would seek him of our own accord. For happiness consists in cleaving to God through the exercise of authentic freedom. Thus, freedom is a decision about self whereby we live our lives either for or against the Good, the Truth, and ultimately God. By using our free will to perform morally good acts, we strengthen and develop our likeness to God. Human freedom is an incomparable source for growth and maturity in holiness. In the full flowering of human freedom we discover the nearness of God. Consequently, Gospel freedom remains essential to closing the distance that impairs so many.

Fourth, *the New Evangelization must address people personally in a way that liberates them from fear.* To some degree, all of us capitulate to the fear of failure, rejection, pain, or death. But how insidiously ignorance of the Gospel and the blackmail of sin keep us fearful of our deepest personal secrets. We subsequently live in fear of telling the truth. We become afraid to be ourselves, fearful that we will not fit in, scared that we will never really belong, that no one will love us. Such fear strikes at the very core of our self-worth and well-being. In turn, our fear of what others think of us paralyzes us when confronted with the antagonism and antipathy of the world. Only a New Evangelization that reactivates the saving words of Jesus Christ — "Do not be afraid" — can in fact save us from all that afflicts and frightens us — especially from within.

And fifth, *the New Evangelization must bring about a profound, personal encounter with the Person of Christ.* This remains the special charge of priests who act *in persona Christi* as the *Directory for the Life and Ministry of Priests* elucidates:

> "The priest must above all revive his faith, his hope, and his sincere love for the Lord in such a way as to be able to present him for the contemplation of the faithful and all men as he truly is: a living and fascinating Person, who loves us more than anyone else because he has given his life for us. At the same time, the priest, conscious that each person is, in diverse ways, looking for a love that is capable of bringing him beyond the anguishes concomitant with human weakness and egoism, and above all with death itself, must proclaim that Jesus Christ is the answer to all these anxieties" (35).

PART ONE:
REFLECTIONS ON THE
SUNDAY GOSPELS

First Sunday of Advent

From Nightmare to Life's Dream
Luke 21:25-28, 34-36

The description we hear from the lips of Jesus this first Sunday of Advent sounds like a nightmare: Omens in the heavens, nations in dismay, roaring oceans, people dying of fright, apocalyptic visions in the sky, the day assaulting us like a weapon and ambushing us like a trap. The only way to escape the horrors of a bad dream is to wake up. And that is why Jesus warns us not to "become drowsy."

In the last days, all the world will cower "in anticipation of what is coming upon the world." This same "anticipation" fills the people waiting for Zechariah outside the temple where the angel is announcing the birth of one who comes to prepare a people fit for the Lord (Lk 1:21, 17). Anticipation characterizes the crowd waiting for Jesus after he heals the Gerasene demoniac (Lk 8:40). A holy regard for anticipation is what distinguishes the vigilant servant from the faithless one in Christ's parable about expecting the Master (Lk 12:35-48). In other words, anticipation can lead us to either fright-filled death, or hope-filled life. What matters now is how we await the Master who comes to heal us and make us a people fit for himself.

However, fear remains a major obstacle to welcoming the Son of Man, who comes in great glory. For example, inside the temple, at the sight of the angel, Zechariah caves in to fear (Lk 1:12). Later on, this fear infects his entire neighborhood (Lk 1:65) as it does the whole population of the Gerasene territory when they witness the healing of the demoniac (Lk 8:37). Clearly, we need something to perfect our anticipation and to greet our *redemption* like the recovered Zechariah (Lk 1:68) and the prophetess Anna (2:38).

The Lord himself furnishes that something. Jesus does so first of all by freeing our hearts from all "carousing and drunkenness and the anxieties of daily life." Jesus addressed these same anxieties in chiding Martha about the "need of only one thing" (Lk 10:42), in counseling his disciples how to remain calm when confronted by enemies (Lk 12:11), and in warning his disciples about the delusion of worry (Lk 12:22-26). Our hearts are made for the "better portion" who is Jesus. He himself supplies the words we need to defend ourselves. He provides for our every need in the world so that we can live wholly for him.

Moreover, Jesus enjoins us to "be vigilant at all times." More than mere attentiveness, this is a summons to a watchfulness that protects us from the hypocrisy of the Pharisees (Lk 12:1), that makes us merciful in dealing with the sins of others (Lk 17:3), and that saves us from the self-importance and treachery of the scribes (Lk 20:46-47). Without such vigilance, we too would fall prey to hypocrisy, ruthlessness, conceit, and deceit.

And Jesus calls us so as to pray to escape tribulations. These words foreshadow the command that the Lord will issue to his sleepy apostles in the garden of Gethsemane (Lk 22:39-46). But it is not enough merely to remain awake; we must not remain lying on the ground, but be alert and on our feet. We are to pray for the strength to "stand before the Son of Man." That is the way the Lord finds us praying at Mass just before we receive Holy Communion. For "what is coming upon the world" is the Lamb of God, who takes away the sins of the world.

Second Sunday of Advent

The Dramatis Personae of the Redemption
Luke 3:1-6

The opening of today's Gospel consists of a catalogue of the names of many of the people who will populate the Passion of Jesus Christ. Their mention adds an air of ominous foreboding to a season that looks forward to so much joy and mirth. Pontius Pilate, Herod, Annas, and Caiaphas conspire to remind us of the outcome of Christ's life even before he is born. Their prominence threatens to fill us with a sense of dread.

Yet, amidst and despite the presaging of so much ultimate treachery, blasphemy, and violence, "the word of God came to John the son of Zechariah in the desert." John the Baptist lights our hope. In calling us to level off the mountains and valleys, to straighten out the winding roads, and to smooth out rough ways, John provides us a clear and sure way to join Jesus on the Way to Calvary. Because we submit to John's baptism of repentance, the Passion is not forbidding but forgiving. The announcement of so many wicked persons serves to make us that much more certain of the redemptive intervention of the merciful Persons of the Blessed Trinity.

The Word of God that comes to John is the same Word that dismisses the saintly Simeon in peace (Lk 2:29). It is the divine voice of election that we will hear at the Transfiguration (Lk 9:35). It is the Word of God's wisdom that Jesus repeats to repudiate the murderous lawyers and Pharisees (Lk 11:49). It is the Word that warns all those who seek to get rich for themselves instead of for God (Lk 12:20). It is the Word that inspires the Psalmist, but that confounds the Sadducees (Lk 20:42). In the same way, God's Word comes to us at this moment of Advent to reassure us of his providence and to confirm his paternal care. By listening closely to this Word and assenting to what God's wisdom reveals, we invest our unfailing trust in God who enables us to recognize Christ at Christmas as Messiah, Lord, and Son. Unlike the dissemblers at the Passion, that is precisely how we confess him.

The forgiveness that remains the goal of John's baptism is just what the identified antagonists of the Passion refuse. But, as Zechariah prophesied earlier, we cannot come to a knowledge of salvation unless we experience the forgiveness of our sins (Lk 1·77). Therefore, Christ will spend his life demonstrating his power and preference to forgive (Lk 5:21-24). The effect of such forgiveness in a believer is the superabundance of love (Lk 7:47). Forgiveness lies at the very heart of authentic Christian prayer (Lk 11:4). Forgiveness is not an isolated act, but a permanent way of life (Lk 17:4). In fact, forgiveness distinguishes the whole of Jesus' life as it becomes his last request before death (Lk 23:34). For nothing can kill forgiveness. Indeed, the offer of Gospel forgiveness remains the preeminent sign that Christ's Resurrection has triumphed over the evil of the world (Lk 24:47).

If we long to incorporate ourselves with all who "shall see the salvation of God," the Gospel calls us step away from the crowd and to turn our back on the majority. Although the two sides stand seven to one, we side with the one, John the Baptist, because he is for the One who is Jesus.

Third Sunday of Advent

Worthiness and the Church
Luke 3:10-18

The crowds from every walk of life come before John the Baptist and ask him: "What then should we do?" Amazingly, John's direct answers restrict themselves to the realm of mere common sense. In sum, he tells the people to share the necessities of life with the needy and not to be underhanded, dishonest, abusive of power, or greedy. This is only the stuff of basic civility, and hardly the hallmark of great holiness. But such fundamental reform remains the first sure step to solid sanctity. Sometimes we need such candor to kick-start conversion.

However, the infallible sign that God's grace is at work in these encounters is the desire, the willingness of the crowds, to seek out God's holy herald in order to become holy themselves. Such a docile approach to the forerunner of Christ leads us out of our selfishness and self-righteousness. The single fact that they accede to such obedience is a definite sign that the Spirit is guiding them to saintliness. In the ministry of John we begin to experience the mediatorial role of the Church.

The dynamic of relying on the one set apart by God, which forms our preparation for the birth of Jesus, poignantly reappears after Christ's Resurrection. When the thousands in Jerusalem hear the post-Pentecost Peter preaching, they become deeply shaken, and they ask Peter and the other apostles: "What are we to do, my brothers?" Peter's instruction is as direct and practical as the Baptist's: "Repent and be baptized, every one of you, in the name of Jesus Christ for the forgiveness of your sins" (Acts 2:38). The more we turn to the Church and her sacraments in holy humility, the more we can turn away from our sins.

As simple and straightforward as it may seem, how radically the people's lives change when someone finally speaks the truth to them. John's words fill the crowds with expectation. As they await the Messiah in their newfound rectitude, they become identified with the expectant Simeon who awaited Israel's consolation (Lk 2:25) and the prophetess Anna whose own words satisfied the expectation of the crowds who looked forward to the deliverance of Jerusalem (Lk 2:38). John the Baptist teaches us not to rest until we have found the true Messiah, and never to compromise the full Truth of Christ (Lk 7:19-28). The expectancy that begins in us at Advent, as it did for these crowds in the desert before the incarnate Jesus appeared, continues even after his death. Joseph of Arimathea, the one who looked expectantly for the reign of God, shows us the form that Advent expectation should take as he approaches Pilate and asks for the body of Jesus (Lk 23:52).

The way to await the Messiah is to listen to the Good News that John preaches and to make it the center of our lives (Lk 16:16). For the Good News we hear from the lips of John is the same as that which resounds from the angels to the shepherds (Lk 2:10), and which Jesus will pronounce as he begins his preaching (Lk 4:18). This is the Good News that Jesus *must* announce (Lk 4:43; 8:1; 20:1), the Good News that proves he is the Messiah (Lk 7:22). The Lord imparts the imperative to proclaim the Good News to us as well (Lk 9:60). It enlivens the Twelve as they set out preaching (Lk 9:6), and it transforms the women as they run from the tomb back to the apostles, the Church (Lk 24:9).

John the Baptist confesses: "I am not worthy to loosen the thongs of his sandals." And neither are we. And so we join our voices with that of the centurion (Lk 7:6) as we come to Jesus in the Eucharist saying, "Lord, I am not worthy to receive you." The worthiness of Jesus will make us worthy. All he asks is that we approach his Church.

Fourth Sunday of Advent

The Greeting That Becomes Blessing
Luke 1:39-45

As the Church draws close to Christmas, the Blessed Virgin Mary sets out in haste for the house of Zechariah. For we need the Mother of God close to us, right with us where we live, in order to benefit from all the inestimable graces of the Incarnation.

What fills Elizabeth with the Holy Spirit and rejoices the child in her womb is the greeting of Mary. The instance of greeting is a privileged and precious occurrence in the Gospel of Luke. The only other recipient of such a godly greeting in the Gospel is the Blessed Virgin Mary herself (Lk 1:28-29). Otherwise, the act of greeting is to play no role in the enterprise of evangelization. Jesus specifically instructs the seventy-two appointed to preach: "Greet no one along the way" (Lk 10:4). In fact, the fierce rebuke that Christ levies against the scribes and Pharisees stems from their churlish attempt at self-promotion by garnering the greetings of others (Lk 11:43; 20:46). Such greetings only exacerbate the hypocrisy, duplicity, and self-righteousness so inimical to the Kingdom.

All of this seems to suggest that no other greeting can ever surpass or take the place of the greeting that the Blessed Virgin Mary herself receives and in turn gives. Her greeting remains efficacious in the Church always. Mary's greeting is the life-giving force of the Holy Spirit. That is why the Hail Mary remains an integral part of Christian spirituality and prayer. The Hail Mary beautifully blends the angel's greeting to Mary with Elizabeth's holy response to the greeting of Mary. The discipline of Advent opens our hearts to embrace that greeting as concretely as Elizabeth received the Mother of God into her home and heart.

If greeting is not the appropriate response to the presence of the Word in the womb of Mary, then what is? Elizabeth shows us when she cries out "in a loud voice" proclaiming the blessedness of Mary and the fruit of her womb. There are others in the Gospel of Luke who cry out in a loud voice: The man in the synagogue with an unclean spirit (Lk 4:33), the Gerasene demoniac (Lk 8:28), the cured leper (Lk 17:15), the disciples on Palm Sunday (Lk 19:37). Their loud voices proclaim that Jesus is the Holy One of God, the Son of the Most High, the one who displays his power in healing the untouchable, the one who comes as King in the name of the Lord. It is only in Jerusalem, at the prompting of scribes and Pharisees so fond of fawning greetings, that the crowds raise their voices to call for Christ's crucifixion (Lk 23:23). But then Jesus himself cries out in a loud voice — a cry by which Jesus commends himself to the same Spirit who greets the Blessed Virgin Mary at the Annunciation.

The abounding joy that Elizabeth and her son experience today is predicated on Mary's belief. The more we use our own voices to proclaim the holiness and mercy of her Son and to commend ourselves to the Holy Spirit to whom Mary gave her complete consent, the more we too will share in the blessedness of the Mother.

Holy Family Sunday

Becoming the Holy Family
Luke 2:41-52

It is strangely consoling that the image of the Holy Family in today's Gospel is not one of a family immersed in perfect bliss. The relative turmoil they experience reassures us that Jesus' family is much like our own. And yet, it is due precisely to the disruption and duress suffered together that the bond of family love is deepened, and so much good is gained.

The evangelist is not being quaint by informing us that Jesus is twelve years old at the time of the finding in the temple. Rather, with the inclusion of this detail, Luke identifies Jesus with the two other times in the Gospel that "twelve years" gets mentioned. The daughter of Jairus whom Jesus raises from the dead is twelve years old (Lk 8:42). The woman who touches the tassel on Jesus' cloak is ill with a hemorrhage for twelve years. In the Gospel, the two stories appear together as one and form a unity of meaning. When Jesus raises the girl to life, he returns her to her parents — an act that reunites their family while perfecting their belief in him. The healing that Christ imparts to the woman makes it possible at last for her to have the family she could never have before because of her affliction. But all the love in her life would continue to be formed by (perhaps) the first man she had ever touched — Jesus.

Jesus at age twelve reminds us that this "lost" boy is the one who will raise us to new life, return us to the Father, and fill us with undying hope to overcome all the loneliness, heartbreak, and despair that bleeds us. The promise of that power is revealed within the embrace of the family.

Mary and Joseph "looked for him" like the crowds that tried to keep him from leaving them (Lk 4:42-43). Jesus responds to their search by telling them that he has been sent to proclaim the Good News to other towns. The two men in dazzling garments say to the women at Jesus' tomb: "Why do you [look for] the living one among the dead?" Our search for Jesus with Mary and Joseph, which is the search for the meaning of our own sonship and daughtership, leads us to an active living of the Gospel and to a sharing in the resurrection that begins in the family.

When Mary and Joseph saw Jesus in the temple interacting with the teachers "they were astonished." "Astonishment" means more than becoming awestruck. Rather, astonishment is an expression of faith and a marveling at the power of God. Jesus' parents experienced astonishment once before in the temple when they went to present their infant Son (Lk 2:33). But such astonishment is not limited to Mary and Joseph. It fills the people who listen to the Christmas preaching of the shepherds (Lk 2:18). It marks those who witness the miracles of Christ (Lk 8:25; 9:43). It overtakes Peter at the empty tomb (Lk 24:12) and the Eleven when the risen Christ appears to them (24:41). In fact, Jesus himself experiences this astonishment when he encounters the surpassing faith of the centurion (Lk 7:9). Within the spiritual womb and the prayer life of the family, faith comes to fruition.

Jesus was obedient to his parents because he recognized their authority as a divinely ordained sharing in the supreme authority of the Father. The Lord in turn imparts this authority to his disciples so that even the demons are obedient to them (Lk 10:17-21). When the disciples rejoice over this fact, Jesus responds in a prayer of praise proclaiming how the Father has revealed great things to children. Obedience to God's authority assures us a lasting place in the Father's family.

Mary, the Mother of God*

Finding Redemption
Luke 2:16-21

As the angel promised (Lk 2:12), the shepherds "found" Mary, Joseph, and Jesus. "Finding" is a significant word in the theology of Luke. The Blessed Virgin Mary is the first to find something — namely, favor with God (Lk 1:30). The ensuing acts of finding in the Gospel in one way or another participate in the divine favor that Mary first found; they are extensions of it. For example, the faith of the centurion that astonishes Jesus (Lk 7:9) models the faith of Mary. The dynamic of finding that forms the three great parables of chapter fifteen reminds us of what the shepherds find today in the arms of Mary: The Lamb of God who seeks us, his lost sheep; God's precious gift who enriches us when we fear being lost in the poverty of sin; the Father's own Son who calls us from death to life.

In another parable (Lk 12:37-48), Jesus praises those servants whom the master finds awake and attentive, awaiting his return. Quite literally, the newborn Master finds these shepherd-servants awake and attending him in the middle of the night. The expectation that delights the Master's incarnate heart is a continuation of the expectant faith that first fills the heart of his Mother.

Because we find Jesus united with Mary, we share the hope of the women at the tomb who find the stone rolled away (Lk 24:2) and of the disciples on the road to Emmaus who return to Jerusalem and find the Eleven (Lk 24:33). We become evangelizers like them and like the shepherds whose proclamation of the Good News enables others to find favor with God.

At the same time, the Mother of God is given to us to be the exemplar of Christian contemplation. "Mary kept all these things, reflecting on them in her heart." The mystery of the Incarnation matures in us through meditation. Joined to Mary's pondering heart (Lk 2:51), we re-

*Editor's note: This Solemnity does not necessarily fall on Sunday.

frain from wandering off into disillusion and dismay. Our union with the heart of the Blessed Virgin Mary enables us to understand, to love, and to live the mysteries of her Son in all their fullness and depth.

Finally, Mary gives her child "the name given him by the angel before he was conceived in the womb." Every time we name Jesus by praying the Holy Name we benefit from the grace of redemption that the name of Jesus signifies. The Lord says, "Whoever receives this child in my name receives me" (Lk 9:48). The Blessed Virgin Mary enables us to welcome Jesus as a little child at Christmas, calling him by name. Just as naming Jesus marks the beginning of his human life, so does it distinguish the revelation of his resurrected life. The risen Jesus instructs the Eleven to preach penance for the remission of sins "in his name" (Lk 24:47). They are able to preach the name of Jesus because of the maternal mediation of Mary.

The shepherds went in haste to Bethlehem. Their action imitates the Blessed Virgin Mary who went in haste to make her visitation of Elizabeth. We in turn go in haste into this New Year filled with the saving Word and the favor of the Holy Spirit that come to us through the Blessed Virgin Mary.

SECOND SUNDAY AFTER CHRISTMAS

BORN FOR THE TRUTH
John 1:1-18

The fullness of Christ that we have received at Christmas is made explicit in today's Gospel. Jesus is the Word, the Creator, the light, the Son who makes us children, flesh dwelling among us, God's glory, grace, and truth.

Christmas is a kind of re-creation. "In the beginning" reminds us of the act of creation recounted in the opening words of Genesis. However, the evangelist John reminds us that the devil "was a murderer from the beginning" (Jn 8:44). Within the peace of Christmas lurks a potential conflict that calls into action the destructive forces of darkness, ignorance, and rejection.

As a result, it is not enough that Jesus be born; he must be *accepted* by us. Later in his life, the Lord will bemoan those who do not accept him but who instead accept the venal praise of others (Jn 5:43-44). Yet, the summons to accept him marks both the beginning and the end of Jesus' life. The night before he dies Jesus assures his disciples that those who accept him accept the Father (Jn 13:20). Therefore, in order to insure that Christmas is for us the kind of beginning that unites us to the re-creating Word and not to the death-dealing devil, we too must be born — born "of God." We must accept Jesus in a way that excepts everything contrary to Christ.

Even now, the Lord's future words to Nicodemus resound in our ears: "You must be born from above" (Jn 3:7). For only such supernatural birth saves us from the snares of death and deception, and makes us partakers of his truth. At the end of his life, Jesus reminds us of the purpose of Christmas: "For this I was born . . . to testify to the truth" (Jn 18:37). The Savior testifies to the truth *in us* when we invest ourselves in the graces of the Incarnation.

The truth that comes to us through Jesus Christ enlightens our lives and makes it possible for us to enact deeds done in God (Jn 3:21). The Truth of Jesus makes our worship pure and perfect (Jn 4:24). The truth sets us free from all that enslaves us (Jn 8:32). The truth consecrates us to God (Jn 17:17, 19). The truth identifies us with Jesus the Truth (Jn 14:6); through the truth Jesus gives us the "power to become children of God."

"All things came to be through him." Jesus' prayer for us at Christmas is the same as his prayer for us before Easter — he yearns for us to come to be fully through him. The source of that fulfillment is the glory that Jesus had with the Father before the world began (Jn 17:5). "We saw his glory" — the glory rooted in allowing Jesus to bring us to new life as he does his friend Lazarus. The voiceless Jesus says to us what he utters to the grieving Martha: "Did I not tell you that if you believe you will see the glory of God?" (Jn 11:40). If we believe, if we live in the truth, if we accept Jesus Christ by surrendering ourselves to be reborn of the Spirit, then we too will see the glory of God. And we will see God's glory in us in the very way that we see it revealed in the human flesh of the incarnate Jesus — we will see God's glory in the holiness of our own physical actions: "By this is my Father glorified, that you bear much fruit and become my disciples" (Jn 15:8).

Epiphany Sunday

Entering the Life of the Church
Matthew 2:1-12

We are told that "on entering the house they [the Magi] saw the child with Mary his mother." This entrance is much like every Christian's entrance into a church. As the *Catechism* instructs us, "to enter into the house of God, we must cross a *threshold*, which symbolizes passing from the world wounded by sin to the world of the new Life to which all men are called" (1186). That entrance, that passage into new Life is what the Epiphany is all about.

Once inside, the Magi do three things. First, they prostrate themselves and give homage to Jesus. Their action foreshadows the faith-filled prostration of many others in the Gospel: The leper who begs Jesus for a cure (Mt 8:2); Jairus as he begs Jesus to raise his daughter to life (Mt 9:18); the disciples who witness Jesus walking on the water (Mt 14:25); the Canaanite woman seeking an exorcism for her daughter (Mt 15:25); the wife of Zebedee seeking the best for her sons (Mt 20:20); the women (Mt 28:9) and the Eleven (Mt 28:17) before the risen Christ. The revelation of Christ at Epiphany becomes real in us when we join the Magi in prostrate homage that expresses our confidence in Jesus' power to heal, enliven, purify, and perfect us.

"They opened their treasures." Jesus tells us that "where your treasure is, there also will your heart be" (Mt 6:21). Thus, the Magi open their hearts to Jesus. They divest themselves of their riches, in a way that the rich young man will refuse, because they prefer to have the treasure in heaven (Mt 19:21) now manifested on earth in the human flesh of Jesus Christ. The mystery of Epiphany calls us to give completely of ourselves so as to be able to possess the treasure of the Kingdom of God (Mt 13:44).

And the Magi "offered him gifts." Their offering foreshadows the offertory of the Mass. When confronted with the hungry five thousand, Jesus will instruct his disciples: "Give them some food yourselves" (Mt 14:16). The gifts offered by the Magi symbolize the gift that Jesus will make of his life — the Paschal Mystery. The offering of the Magi expresses

35

the way that Christians enter in and participate in the offering of Christ's Body and Blood in the Eucharist. As we worship the Body of Christ with the Magi, our offering transforms us into the Body of Christ.

Like Herod, we may feel some hesitation about the Epiphany. "He was greatly troubled." This expression of distress is used only one other time in the Gospel of Matthew: When the disciples see Jesus walking on the water (Mt 14:26). In other words, to be troubled indicates a deficiency of faith — a deficiency that is overcome when we enter the house where Jesus is present. Our union with him there then sends us forth "by another way." And for this way we need not provide for ourselves (Mt 14:16) because the power of Christ, manifested today, will keep us.

"They were overjoyed." Their joy matches that of those who live the beatitudes (Mt 5:12), who find a lost sheep (Mt 18:13), who industriously serve the Master (Mt 25:21, 23), and who look for Jesus crucified (Mt 28:8). In short, the joy of Epiphany is the vocation of the Christian.

THE BAPTISM OF THE LORD

WHY JESUS GETS BAPTIZED
Luke 3:15-16, 21-22

The logical question today is: Why does Jesus allow himself to be baptized? Being sinless, he obviously has no need of baptism's redemptive effects. But, as the Gospel makes clear, when Jesus gets baptized, we become the beneficiaries of the graces that flow from this sacred action, especially in three ways.

First of all, the baptism of Jesus is not a private affair between God and himself, but rather a communal action that unites believers in hope. Luke tells us that "all the people had been baptized," and that the baptized Jesus was praying with them. In the midst of this praying sacred assembly, "heaven was opened" upon the People of God. The hope-filled "expectation" of the Messiah that fills the hearts of the holy ones in the Gospel — Simeon (Lk 2:25), Anna (Lk 2:38), John the Baptist (Lk 7:19-20), and Joseph of Arimathea (Lk 23:51) — is met in this dawning.

From this open heaven Satan will fall (Lk 10:18) and to this heaven the risen Jesus will ascend (Lk 24:51). In this heaven great signs will appear (Lk 21:11), and from this heaven the Father will send an angel to strengthen his Son in agony (Lk 22:43). For this heaven is the source of the disciples' true treasure (Lk 12:33; 18:22) where they find their own names inscribed (Lk 10:20). Moreover, this heaven is the place of jubilation over just one repentant sinner (Lk 15:7). The crowd of repentant baptized today must cause heaven powerful joy indeed. The people partake of this joy because of the hope that unites them in prayer to Christ.

Jesus is baptized also to perfect our faith. "The Holy Spirit descended upon him." Only one other time do we read about something "descending" in the Gospel (and it too involves water) — the windstorm that descends on the lake (Lk 8:22-25). This descent terrifies the disciples until Jesus stills the storm. He then asks them, "Where is your faith?" In both cases, the heavenly descent is meant to fill those present with a faith that leads to a more profound belief in the Lord.

The baptism of Jesus is the beginning of our being baptized with the Holy Spirit and fire. Jesus says: "I have come to set the earth on fire, and how I wish it were already blazing! There is a baptism with which I must be baptized" (Lk 12:49-50). The more we unite ourselves to the baptism of Jesus that begins today but that culminates on the cross, the more our hearts burn within us with unquenchable faith, like the disciples on the road to Emmaus (Lk 24:32).

And the baptism of Jesus invites us to a deeper intimacy of love with the Blessed Trinity. We hear the voice of the Father professing his love for his Son in the union of the Holy Spirit. What the Father declares to his Son — "With you I am well pleased" — is meant for us, his disciples, as well. This declaration is made by the host of angels to the shepherds on Christmas night when they sing: "Peace to those on whom [God's] favor rests" (Lk 2:14) — a favor in which we participate every time we proclaim the Gloria. It pleases the Father to reveal the things of heaven to the merest children (Lk 10:21) and to give his little flock the Kingdom of God (Lk 12:32). And that is precisely what the Father's love does for us today in the baptism of his Son.

SECOND SUNDAY IN ORDINARY TIME

DOING WHAT JESUS TELLS US
John 2:1-11

In the beginning was the Word, and the beginning of Jesus' ministry is marked by "the beginning of his signs." In this beginning Jesus devotes himself to satisfying the thirst of his fellow wedding guests; at the end of his life the Bridegroom cries out from the cross, "I thirst" (Jn 19:28). In both instances Christ's end is the same: To reveal his "glory" and to deepen his disciples' belief in him. For the glory of Jesus is men and women fully alive.

Divine glory appears as the communication of the very goodness of God. With the Incarnation of Jesus Christ, we understand this glory to be nothing less than the holiness of God revealed in creation. Perhaps that is why Jesus uses so much of creation — one hundred twenty gallons worth! — to manifest his holiness/glory. Jesus means for the goodness of glory to be overabundant. There is enough for everyone to imbibe.

In order to partake of this bounty of glory, we must obey the Mother of God and do whatever Jesus tells us. It includes three things. First we are to "fill the jars with water." This action and the act of filling the baskets after the multiplication of the loaves (Jn 6:13) have sacramental overtones. The water reminds us of baptism; the bread reminds us of the Eucharist. As Jesus begins his signs he shows us the way to live our faith by receiving the sacred signs of the Sacraments. Through the created matter of the Sacraments of the Church, God perfects us, his creatures, in holiness. Participating in the sacramental life of the Church is the way we glorify God.

Jesus commands us, "Draw some out." As the story of the woman at the well makes plain, the act of drawing water can be both onerous and bothersome (Jn 4:7, 11, 15). In this case, the waiters probably see it as a futile waste of time, since they presume it's tasteless water from a washing jar. However, "the headwaiter tasted the water that had become wine without knowing where it came from." Jesus commands us to draw water because things are not always what they seem. The act of drawing

39

opens our eyes and refashions our will. The one who asks us for a drink of water may himself be living water. The jar that the Lord instructs us to draw from may in fact be a fountain leaping up to provide eternal life.

Our obedience to the instructions of Jesus saves us from presumption and renews our hope. Why should we trust our own close-minded judgment? We do not even know where the wind comes from (Jn 3:8). Like the people of Jerusalem, we too readily settle for false conclusions about Jesus and his origins (Jn 7:27-28). Only the judgment and witness of Jesus are trustworthy because, as he declares, "I know where I came from" (Jn 8:14). This knowledge defies the self-righteous Pharisees (Jn 9:29-30) as well as the distraught and fearful Pilate (Jn 19:9). However, those who listen to the voice of Jesus and obey him with confidence know where the water of salvation comes from — despite appearances to the contrary. As they draw from that Well, they themselves are transformed.

And finally, Jesus says: "Take it to the headwaiter." This taking is an act of charity that shares in the sacrifice of the Eucharist: "Take and drink." Nicodemus takes a hundred pounds of myrrh and aloes to the body of Jesus out of love and reverence (Jn 19:39). The risen Jesus tells Thomas to take his finger and put it in the wounds of his Body (Jn 20:27). As we take what we are told, Jesus unites us to his Body. The headwaiter calls the wine "good" — a term in the Gospel of John otherwise reserved exclusively to Jesus himself (Jn 1:46; 7:12; 10:11, 14). We take and partake of the goodness of Jesus — Holy Communion.

THIRD SUNDAY IN ORDINARY TIME

HEARING AND FULFILLMENT
Luke 1:1-4, 4:14-21

The Church is blessed with yet another beginning with today's Gospel from the beginning of Luke. The evangelist refers to his Gospel as "a narrative of the events that have been fulfilled among us." A narrative is a literary presentation of a complete action. Accordingly, Gospel episodes are more than mere stories told to impart information and to elicit emotional response. Rather, the narrative dynamic of the Gospel continues the redemptive gestures of Jesus Christ in our time. Through literary reenactment, Gospel narrative makes present for every reader/hearer Christ's saving activity. Now the events of salvation have become Word without losing any of their efficacy.

As a result, the Gospel bears witness, not only to what Jesus *has done*, but to what he *is doing* now. Like the "most excellent Theophilus," — which means "loved by God" — for anyone who disposes himself by faith to the literary action of the Gospel, the Gospel becomes a source of salvific encounter with Jesus Christ here and now.

Luke has written down the events of the Gospel accurately, in an orderly sequence so that the disciple "may realize the certainty of the teachings you have received." Therefore, the receiver of the Gospel must show the same attention and diligence in reading/hearing the Gospel as Luke engaged in writing it. Jesus makes this plain when he enters the synagogue, proclaims the Word of God, and ends his recitation with the declaration: "Today this Scripture passage is fulfilled in your hearing."

The fulfillment of the Gospel in our lives depends on our hearing it attentively, listening to it lovingly, and responding to it faithfully. For then Christ's Words will produce the same joy for us as Mary's greeting gives to Elizabeth and John the Baptist (Lk 1:44). That is why Jesus repeatedly insists, "Whoever has ears to hear ought to hear" (Lk 8:8, 14:35); "Pay attention to what I am telling you" (Lk 9:44).

Ironically, the fulfillment in our hearing also involves our seeing: "The eyes of all in the synagogue looked intently at him." For the fulfillment in Christ takes effect at the moment of its proclamation, yet it enfolds systematically over the course of Jesus' ministry. To witness this promised fulfillment, we must continue to keep our eyes intently fixed on Jesus at every moment. There is a certain urgency about this, for Jesus will lament: "If this day you only knew what makes for peace — but now it is hidden from your eyes" (Llt 10:42) When we lose focus of the Lord in our life, the fulfillment he professes loses its force for us personally.

However, as we join the faithful in the synagogue who fix their eyes on Jesus, we become like Simeon in the temple who proclaims, "My eyes have seen your salvation" (Lk 2:30). As we reverently listen to the Words of Jesus, like the disciples on the road to Emmaus (Lk 24:31), our eyes will be opened to the resurrected power of Jesus Christ in our midst.

Then we will see how what Jesus promises he brings to pass. Jesus preaches the Good News to the poor like the widow whose living of the Gospel leads her to give all she owns to God (Lk 21:3). Jesus gives liberty to captives like the good thief (Lk 23:40-43); gives sight to the blind (Lk 7:21; 18:35); and Jesus frees the oppressed like the Gerasene demoniac (Lk 8:38). In turn, he asks us to live the fulfillment he makes accessible by sharing the anointing of the Spirit of the Lord that we have received in baptism with others: "When you hold a banquet, invite the poor, the crippled, the lame, the blind" (Lk 14:13). Then they will realize the certainty of Christ's teaching and the fulfillment of his preaching.

FOURTH SUNDAY IN ORDINARY TIME

AMAZEMENT AND GRACE
Luke 4:21-30

After the finding in the temple, Luke tells us that Jesus advanced in favor (grace) (Lk 2:52). Today in the synagogue we witness the fruit of that advancement in the people who "were amazed at the gracious words that came from his mouth." Several times in the Gospel, speaking causes amazement: Zechariah's naming of his son (Lk 1:63); the preaching of the shepherds (Lk 2:18); Simeon's canticle (Lk 2:33); when the Lord stills the storm (Lk 8:24-25); casts out a demon (Lk 11:14); confounds the spies sent by the scribes and high priests (Lk 20:26); and addresses the Eleven (Lk 24:41). In sum, amazement appears when words are used to bless, to preach, to proclaim God's power, and to offer his mercy under the inspiration of grace.

It is right that the congregation "spoke highly" of Jesus. For in this acclaim they join their voices to the others in the Gospel who praise the goodness of God manifested in Jesus Christ: The paralyzed man (Lk 5:25); the crowds who witness the raising of the widow's son (Lk 7:16); the stooped woman (Lk 13:13); the leper (Lk 17:15, 18); the blind man (Lk 18:43); and the centurion at the cross (Lk 23:47). In each instance, the utterance of praise acknowledges the greatness of Christ's compassion — an undeserved grace and favor given with utter generosity and at great risk.

And yet, how quickly this amazement turns to "fury." The people's perfidy proceeds from their pettiness: They will not accept that Jesus is anything more than "the son of Joseph." However, Jesus identifies himself as a "prophet" (Lk 13:33). The crowd in Nain who witness the raising of the widow's son eagerly acknowledge Jesus as "a great prophet" (Lk 7:16) as do the disciples on the road to Emmaus (Lk 24:19). In other words, those who avail themselves of the mercy and life-giving power of Jesus Christ delight to proclaim him prophet. Conversely, those who remain caught up in their own self-righteousness and presumption disdain and condemn Jesus the Prophet (Lk 7:39; 22:64).

Therefore, if we are to benefit from the gracious Words of Jesus, we have to make a choice. The people of the synagogue chose to rise up, drive Jesus out of town, and lead him to the brow of the hill. These are deadly choices. Before too long, the entire assembly of the Sanhedrin will also rise up and lead Jesus to Pilate (Lk 23:1). Moreover, Jesus seems to recall this act of being driven out in the parable of the tenants that he tells before he dies (Lk 20:12,15). But those who reject the Good News of Jesus will themselves be driven out (Lk 13:28; 19:45). And, in leading Jesus to the hill, the people's action is nothing short of diabolical as it mirrors the moves of the Tempter (Lk 4:5, 9).

To help us, then, to make the right choice, Jesus himself makes a choice. He chooses to lead us to the top of Calvary where he will die for our sins. He chooses to drive out hatred and evil by his self-sacrifice. And he chooses to be raised up on the cross so that we will be raised up in his Resurrection.

Fifth Sunday in Ordinary Time

Lowered Nets and Uplifted Lives
Luke 5:1-11

The crowd presses in on Jesus and listens to the Word of God. The fishermen, on the other hand, remain completely absorbed in the tasks of their trade: They are washing their nets, seemingly oblivious to the Lord and his Word. They are caught up in everyday affairs instead of attending to the Master of the universe who stands in their midst. So Jesus makes the bold move of stepping into one of the boats where he finishes one discourse and then begins a brand new one just for the fishermen "after he had finished speaking."

Christ makes three commands of us. First we are to put out into deep water. How easy it is to limit our life to what is shallow, superficial, and safe. Then Jesus Christ is just another voice in the crowd. But when committed to the deep water of faith-living, we cannot take our eyes off Jesus who is as close to us as the next bench in the boat. We need to avail ourselves of silence and contemplation in order to appreciate the presence of Christ in our life and to put out of our life all self-serving distraction.

The Lord commands: "Lower your nets for a catch." Peter complies, but his assent is begrudging. His obedience remains imperfect because he lacks true conviction in the divine Providence that prompts the command. He thinks he knows better. And so often do we. In commanding us to lower our nets, the Lord affords us the chance to demonstrate our confidence in God's merciful wisdom. When we symbolically lower our nets through trust, then Jesus lifts us out of ourselves, and gives us the graced ability to respond to the will of God in a way that exceeds our natural capacity.

Trust in Christ's command makes the fishermen instantaneously rich. For them the vast catch of fish was like cashing in a winning lottery ticket. In the blink of an eye, they became blessed with wealth, security, prestige, leisure, power.

But Peter recognizes that there is much more than many fish at

45

stake here. He immediately interprets the great take as a token of God's lavish favor of those who are not worthy of it. And so, Peter falls to his knees, confessing his sinfulness In his posture, Peter resembles the leper, the demoniac, the synagogue leader, and the woman with the hemorrhage, who all fall to their knees in order to receive the healing they sorely seek.

However, God permits us to see our sins only to bring about in us a deeper confidence in his mercy and compassion. Thus, Jesus issues his third command: "Do not be afraid." In the Gospel of Luke, those who are "afraid" are those who witness the miraculous power of Jesus Christ (Lk 5:26; 7:16; 8:25; 8:35-37; 9:34; 24:5; 24:37). The consoling Words of Jesus transform us who so often feel like outcasts into those who cast out their nets to draw others into the deep water and the living fount of grace.

Sixth Sunday in Ordinary Time

The Blessings That Lead to Blessedness
Luke 6:17, 20-26

This sermon on the plain is the first message that the Twelve hear Jesus preach upon their selection as apostles (Lk 6:12-16). Their presence at the event helps us to understand the full import of Christ's message. In the first part of the Gospel, the apostles appear in a positive light, accompanying the Lord in his proclamation of the Good News (Lk 8:1), and then going off on their own to minister with the very power and authority of Christ (Lk 9:1).

But then they seem to take a turn for the worse. The Twelve want Jesus to dismiss the crowd of five thousand instead of trusting the Lord to multiply loaves and fishes. The Twelve fail to understand Christ's prediction of his Passion (Lk 18:31). When Satan enters Judas, the evangelist goes out of his way to remind us that Judas is one of the Twelve (Lk 22:3). Similarly, it is this one of the Twelve who leads the crowd to Jesus for betrayal (Lk 22:47).

These four occasions of failure seem to correspond to the four situations that visit woe upon us. Woe to those rich like Judas with his thirty pieces of blood-money silver. Woe to those who are so filled that their self-satiation makes them ungenerous and uncreative when confronted with the hunger of others. In the same way, it is something of the apostles' self-contentment and false sense of security that turns their denseness about Christ's Passion prediction into weeping and grief. And certainly the crowd must have been speaking well of Judas as he led them to the garden to betray and arrest Jesus Christ.

In other words, the key to successful apostleship lies in being poor, hungry, mournful, and hated. The sign that Christ's messiahship is authentic is that the poor have the Good News preached to them (Lk 7:22). The poor are to be the preferred guests when we give a reception (Lk 14:13). The self-emptied poor enjoy welcome in the bosom of Abraham (Lk 16:23). Self-imposed poverty that assists the poor is a prerequisite for discipleship (Lk 18:22; 19:8). For only such self-

47

abandoned poverty gives the greatest witness to the power of living by faith (Lk 21:1-4).

Jesus calls the hungry blessed because their need disposes them to receive the plenty of God of which the Blessed Virgin Mary sings in her Magnificat: "The hungry he has filled with good things" (Lk 1:53).

In the same way, weeping makes us especially receptive of God's mercy. The Gospel is full of examples of those blessed as a result of their weeping: The widow of Nain (Lk 7:13); the sinful woman (Lk 7:38); Jesus himself (Lk 19:41); the women on the way of the cross (Lk 23:27); and, in a special way, Peter the apostle (Lk 22:62).

Christians regard being hated as a mark of blessedness in fulfillment of the Benedictus: "He promised . . . salvation from our enemies and from the hand of all who hate us " (Lk 1:70-71). Enduring denouncement and insult leads us to leap for joy on that day in the same way that John the Baptist leapt in the womb of his mother (Lk 1:41, 44). The exclusion we experience from others only incorporates us more securely into our communion with Christ — so much so that, as true apostles, we can love our enemies and do good to those who hate us (Lk 6:27-35).

Seventh Sunday in Ordinary Time

Jesus' Life and Our Moral Greatness
Luke 6:27-38

What is the difference between the altruism of sinners and the charity of God? What distinguishes well-intentioned philanthropy from life-giving divine love? That is what Jesus seeks to make clear in his instruction to his disciples today. The charity of Jesus Christ goes beyond the limitations of mere justice. Divine charity does not quit whenever fairness flags in others' dealings with us — it increases! Thus, Christian goodness must be shown in particular to those who hate, who mistreat, who strike, who deprive, and who abuse our generosity. How is this possible?

The memory of our own neediness, powerlessness, weakness, and unworthiness informs the standard we use in relating to others. For we cannot forget how the merciful Father enfolds us with his kindness despite our ingratitude and wickedness. As a result, the one possessed of divine charity harbors no egocentric regard for self. Rather, the Christian transfigured by divine charity remains wholly fixed on the good of the other, sharing in the other's need in its ultimate meaning as would a true friend. In this way, the rabid tyranny of limited justice becomes the ravishing freedom of divine love.

Of course, Christ's commands — stop judging, stop condemning, forgive, and give — are not the abstract, idealistic injunctions of a moralizing dictator. Rather, they are grace-filled means of realizing the universal call to holiness. We can do what Christ instructs us because Jesus himself fulfills these commands first in his own human life, especially in his Passion.

Christ proves how possible it is to love our enemies through the love he shows to those who crucify him. Although the crowd curses and jeers him, Jesus refuses to retaliate. Rather, he blesses them, lifting his voice to heaven in prayer for those who mistreat him. He does good to those who hate him by petitioning for their forgiveness. He offers his hands and his feet to be nailed to those who strike him on the face. To those who strip him for crucifixion Jesus does not withhold his tunic. To the good thief who asks to be remembered in Christ's Kingdom, Jesus gives paradise.

Jesus can do all this because he lives fully and completely out of the love the Father has for him. No wonder, then, that Christ's directions today so much resemble the petitions of the Lord's Prayer. The more we pray "Our Father" the more do we relinquish the craving to impose our own judgments and sense of superiority on others. When we pray "thy kingdom come, thy will be done" we receive the grace to live without condemning others. We can forgive because of the way that Jesus teaches to pray for the ability. And as we ask the Father to give us our daily bread, we grow in our eagerness to give in kind to others. No wonder, as well, that the reward for loving our enemies is the privilege of being children of the Most High.

The moral greatness of the Gospel may seem daunting unless we remember that Jesus lived for us and not for himself. He thereby empowers us to live in him everything that he did and desired, and Jesus lives it in us. That is the overflowing measure that Jesus pours into our laps and into our souls when we live according to no lesser measure.

EIGHTH SUNDAY IN ORDINARY TIME

THE FULLNESS OF THE HEART
Luke 6:39-45

The Lord gives us a lesson on growth in perfection that emphasizes appropriate guidance, rigorous self-knowledge, and superb fruitfulness. In singling out these aspects of human maturity, Jesus indicates that how we listen, how we self-efface, and how we act contribute to the kind of "fullness of the heart" from which we speak.

Such reconditioning and replenishing of the human heart lies behind the entire mission of Jesus. His forerunner, John the Baptist, was raised up to convert hearts so as to dispose people to receive the Lord (Lk 1:17). In fact, everlasting life depends on loving God with all our heart (Lk 10:27). For wherever our treasure is, there is our heart (Lk 12:34). When Jesus Christ is our treasure, then our hearts will burn with the fullness of his love like the hearts of the disciples on the road to Emmaus (Lk 24:32).

How then do we get goodness in our heart so as to become a good person? It means like Mary, the sister of Martha, choosing the better portion, which is self-abandonment to Jesus (Lk 10:42). For, as Jesus reminds one of the ruling class, no one is good but God alone (Lk 18:19). However, the more we capitalize on the investment of Jesus Christ to us, symbolized by the parable of the sums of money, the more does the Master call us "good" (Lk 19:17). That goodness transforms every aspect of our life, and keeps our heart filled with hope, fixed upon Jesus even after his death. Like Joseph of Arimathea, who is described as good and holy (Lk 23:50), we want nothing but to be one with the Body of Jesus, which means to be united to the divine Person of the Son that it expresses.

The key remains an unrelenting, rectified self-perception — a self-knowledge that sees through all the self-deception, contriving, rationalization, and self-righteousness that would conspire to keep our life cloaked in secrecy and unaccountability. For the Lord Jesus can see beyond all our self-willed hypocrisy just as he perceived the duplicity of the spies sent by the scribes and high priests to trap him in his speech (Lk 20:23).

When we give ourselves fully to Christ, Christ gives himself fully to us and thereby reveals ourselves to ourselves. We can see ourselves with the Lord's own penetrating, purifying vision, and we can see beyond the snares and lures of the world's seduction and compromise.

The Christian must bear good fruit, even as Mary bore fruit in her womb (Lk 1:42). For every tree that is not fruitful will be cut down (Lk 3:9). Therefore, our hearts must remain attentive to the seed of the Word for the guidance and training that yields a hundredfold harvest (Lk 8:8, 15).

The resulting "fullness" of the Christian heart can be compared to the twelve baskets of food left over from the feeding of the five thousand (Lk 9:17) and the abundant food enjoyed by the servants at the home of the prodigal son's father. In other words, the fullness of the heart is a kind of feast that flows from Jesus, the Bread of Life. When we live trusting his guidance and obedient to his mercy, then our mouth is ready to speak to God's glory with all our heart.

Ninth Sunday in Ordinary Time

Presence in the Word
Luke 7:1-10

What was the basis for the centurion's extraordinary confidence in sending the elders to Jesus with the request for him to come and save his sick slave? Something compelled the centurion to believe that Jesus would actually change his itinerary and go out of his way to heed the petition of a man who was not even a Jew.

Obviously, the centurion was keenly attuned to Jesus and devoted to his words and deeds. An earlier time when Jesus was in Capernaum (the centurion's home), Christ left the crowds spellbound by his teaching (Lk 4:32). During that same visit, Jesus cured a demoniac in the synagogue (Lk 4:36). Moreover, the centurion may also have heard of the day that Jesus forgave the sins of the paralytic and healed him (Lk 5:25). What unites these three incidents is the manifestation of Jesus' authority. As a man of authority himself, the centurion reveres the power he sees displayed in Christ, and believes it will be the key to the healing of his servant.

However, the elders think Jesus should come because the centurion is "deserving." To be deserving is not an enviable status in the Gospel of Luke. The unfaithful servant deserves to be flogged (Lk 12:48). The prodigal son readily confesses that he know longer deserves to be regarded as a son (Lk 15:18, 21). Pilate admits that Jesus has done nothing deserving of death (Lk 23:15), and yet he nonetheless delivers Jesus up to crucifixion. It seems that Jesus' motive in going with them must go beyond the appearance of "deserving."

We are told that Jesus "went with them"— the phrase that is used to describe the risen Christ walking with the disciples on the road to Emmaus. Which means that this encounter with Jesus is meant to deepen the faith of those who walk with him.

The centurion sends his friends to Jesus asking only for his presence in his Word. "When Jesus heard this he was amazed" — the only time that Jesus is amazed in Luke. The centurion asks for the Word of which others will be ashamed (Lk 9:26). Christ's is the Word that will not pass away (Lk 21:33). Its remembrance reduces Peter to tears after his denial of Jesus (Lk 22:61-62). Christ's words come back to the women at the tomb to rescue them from their fear (Lk 24:8). But at this moment, Christ's Word is the healing force for the sick slave.

This leads Jesus to exclaim that he has never found such faith. But he will again soon: In the sinful woman (Lk 7:50); in the woman with a hemorrhage (Lk 8:48); and in the leper (Lk 17:19). Will he find faith in us?

Unfortunately, the test of faith does not seem to take in the elders. Soon they will reject Jesus (Lk 9:22), accompany Judas to arrest him (Lk 22:52), and put him on trial (Lk 22:66). We can hardly believe our ears when they ask Jesus in Jerusalem: "By what authority are you doing these things?" (Lk 20:2). They were there; they should know. But they have since sold out to an inferior authority, which leaves us stupefied and amazed. But even this strengthens our faith as it prompts us to pray that Jesus will not give us what we deserve, but that he will nonetheless come to us. We have confidence in his Word.

First Sunday of Lent

The Triumph of the Father's Love
Luke 4:1-13

The Holy Spirit leads Jesus into a trying, contrary, lifeless, impossible place. But in the desperation of the desert Jesus will come to terms with the providence of his Father's love. The verses that immediately precede this passage constitute the genealogy of Jesus from his foster father Joseph to Adam. The long genealogy is a great testament of paternal solicitude and divine care. As the Spirit ushers Jesus seemingly alone into the yawning, sterile expanse of the desert, he is in fact enveloped by the seamless ancestry of godliness and faith. And so are we as we enter into the holy season of Lent.

Here in the desert the Son of God is set apart to discover the fullness of the Father's providential love. The devil's temptations serve to deepen the realization that Jesus' relationship with his Father defines his vocation, his mission, his destiny as Messiah. In the same way, it is through the purifying trial of temptations that we come to terms with our own human vocation and the splendor of our dignity. Jeopardy makes us jealous of it.

Temptations remain useful in disabusing us of false notions, anxiety, impetuousness, reluctance, and impulse. And those closest to God can be certain that Satan has it in for them, for only the holy ones qualify as a kind of trophy or prize for the evil one. The devil need not expend any effort on those intent on losing their souls by their own initiative. Even still, the evil one remains stingy in the way he administers temptations; he uses no more ammunition than absolutely necessary.

Thus, in the attempt to get Jesus to disown his Father, the devil first addresses his hunger — the most basic human need. When that fails, he proceeds to a more sophisticated human need: For power, privilege, and prestige. At wit's end, the devil must ultimately resort to his most subtle and devious device: He tempts Jesus to risk his life to coerce the Father into demonstrating his love and protection. But it is not yet the time for Jesus to lay down his life. And on Calvary, when that time at last comes, the Father will permit the death of his Son; in fact, he will will it. For it is the will of the Father to demonstrate his infinite love for his Son, not in saving him from death, but in raising him to new life from the tomb. Only the heart of Jesus, perfectly conformed to the will of the Father, could embrace this truth in creative obedience.

How easy it is for us, though, to succumb to the seductive yet pernicious wiles of the devil. What depth of rectitude, what profundity of grace does the Christian soul require to perceive the divine rationale behind suffering. How many of us would recklessly throw ourselves off the parapet in a dare to God to display his supernatural care. It is the devil's way of getting us to recreate God and his love according to our own image and understanding. How many of us accuse God of negligence when a supernatural hand does not miraculously materialize to snatch us from the various comedowns of life. The temptation to provoke the Father's love is really a temptation to blasphemy.

In the end, the temptations are about letting God the Father love us in his perfect, predetermined way. Because that is what is best for us, no matter how much the anguish of the desert may inveigle us otherwise. If we hold fast to that hope, the devil will depart from us for a time — to reappear again only at Christ's Passion. But then we are primed for the triumph of the Father's love.

Second Sunday of Lent

The Transfixing Transfiguration
Luke 9:28b-36

Peter, James, and John are present with Jesus at the miraculous catch of fish (Lk 5:10) and at the raising of Jairus' daughter (Lk 8:54). These miracles manifest the magnificence of God's mercy. They caution us not to be quick at jumping to conclusions — things are not always what they seem. An empty depth of sea or the lifeless body of a little girl can reveal the resplendent glory of God himself if Jesus Christ is present to them. Now Jesus leads Peter, James, and John to the top of a mountain to give them a transfixing glimpse of God's mercy before the refulgence of the Resurrection.

Luke stresses how Christ's Transfiguration first appeared in his face. In a few short verses we will be told that this is the face that Jesus sets toward Jerusalem (Lk 9:51) to meet his death on a different summit. Human beings have the compulsion to look each other in the face so as to enter into the other's mind and soul. The face is the most fundamental and original way for people to relate to each other. Throughout our lives, we rely on face-to-face contact to deepen interpersonal communion. As we relate to others via facial communication we at the same time see ourselves reflected in the face of the one we love. What Jesus reveals in his transfigured face is our ultimate destiny. To achieve it, we must not take our eyes off Jesus. To this end, we too now set our face toward Jerusalem.

We are told that Christ's clothing became like lightning. The shepherds at the birth of Jesus were the first to be struck by the glory of God that shone around them (Lk 2:9). But now that brilliance proceeds from and leads back to the transfigured Body of Christ that expresses the divine Person of God's Son. Soon the disciples will experience a related theophany when they see Satan fall from the sky "like lightning" (Lk 10:18). Just as Jesus seems to be transformed into splendor, so is our body to be full of light (Lk 11:36). What the apostles witness now will reappear in the day of the Son of Man which will be like lightning (Lk 17:24). For the moment, Christ's dazzling clothes clue us into the coming of the Resurrection. That is why the two angels at Jesus' tomb are dressed the same way (Lk 24:4).

The apostles are also transfixed by the cloud — yet another instrument of the second coming of Christ (Lk 21:27). However, the cloud also links us to a crucial moment in the past. Just as the power of the Most High once overshadowed the Blessed Virgin Mary at the Annunciation (Lk 1:35), so does it now overshadow these three. In a way, the Transfiguration is a kind of re-conception for the apostles. In a new and transfiguring manner, they carry Jesus' life within them, anticipating the rebirth of all at Christ's Resurrection. The Father's voice beckons them to live in obedience to this mystery.

We may find it horrifying when Herod sends Jesus back to Pontius Pilate dressed in a magnificent robe (Lk 23:11) because of the way it apes Christ's dazzling clothes at the Transfiguration. But for those who believe, Herod's attempt at humiliation becomes a private consolation. The sight of the bedazzling Christ carries us back to the top of that mountain. Once again we are assured that we share Christ's mind, that our body and soul are infused with his enlightening might, and that we are one with Christ in his love of the Father. We are ready for the Passion.

THIRD SUNDAY OF LENT

REPENTANCE AND RESPONSIBILITY
Luke 13:1-9

A consciousness consumed with justice instead of love is quick to conclude that suffering, hardship, and distress are the warranted punishments meted out to sinners. Accordingly, such a mindset supposes — presumptuously — that the absence of disaster in one's life signifies the nonexistence of personal sin. Hence, when one experiences no catastrophe there is no need for contrition. It is so easy to get caught up in such a facile and fractured way of viewing the world. In this Gospel Jesus addresses all those who look for quick, easy, gimmicky explanations of the enigmas of the world and of life.

What the Lord reveals is that true repentance remains the key to understanding everything because sin impairs our very ability to reason. If we do not repent, we will perish. This is what the prodigal son realizes in the most desperate moment of his self-imposed exile (Lk 15:17). The only way home, the only way back to life and the meaning of life is through repentance. With a repentant heart, he makes his way back to his father's home.

The call to repentance is not new in this Gospel. John the Baptist proclaimed it (Lk 3:3, 8). To the contestative Pharisees Christ declared the repentance of others as the motive for his coming. For such repentance rejoices the holy inhabitants of heaven (Lk 15:7). No wonder the risen Jesus commissions the Eleven to make repentance the heart of their preaching to all the nations (Lk 24:47).

It is too easy to think that the Siloam tower fell on the eighteen because they were the most "guilty" — that they had it coming to them. For when a truly "guilty" person does appear at the feet of Jesus, weeping and anointing his feet (Lk 7:37-38), the Lord forgives her on account of her great love. Therefore, the state of being guilty is not fatal; rejecting the mandates of love is.

That is why in the parable Jesus does not side with the owner of the orchard who looks for a quick and easy fix for the problem of his barren fig tree: "Cut it down." God rejects such a simplistic solution when it comes to the fruitlessness of our own lives. But in the process, it puts a certain onus on us — the onus of living responsibility and in repentance. We must show to Jesus, by the integrity of our living, the same confident love that the sinful woman once displayed to him.

Lent is a time to cultivate the ground of our souls in the same way that the man in the Gospel dug deeply to lay a foundation for his house (Lk 6:48). Such cultivation means living rooted in the truth and the goodness of God. If we avoid this kind of digging, then we shall be doomed to dig ditches like the irresponsible manager (Lk 16:3), i.e., we will perish. In the process, we must not overlook the need for manure to make our tree fruitful. Sometimes the most unpleasant, contrary, repelling things enrich our life the most.

The diligent act of tending to the tree of our soul fills our life with an intentionality that dispels all the punditry and quackery of the world. And the same time, it fills us with gratitude that God is not as dismissive towards us in our sin as we often are regarding the plight of others.

FOURTH SUNDAY OF LENT

WHY JESUS EATS WITH SINNERS
Luke 15:1-3, 11-32

The contentious Pharisees and scribes complain about Jesus eating with sinners. To understand why Jesus eats with sinners is to know the Father. Yet, they cannot comprehend Christ's rationale, and they refuse to give Jesus the benefit of the doubt. Similarly, we often have a hard time understanding God the Father. We often rely only on our own limited human experiences of fatherhood in order to make a judgment about the way God the Father should be and act. But the Fatherhood of God transcends human fatherhood, for no one is father as God is Father. The only way Christ's critics can understand his motives for welcoming sinners is by coming to know the Father.

Every single aspect of Christ's earthly life is revelation of the Father. The parable reveals the unique properties of divine Fatherhood. If we long to know who God the Father is and how God is Father, we simply need pay close attention.

The parable first confronts us with the awful truth about ourselves. Because of fallen human nature, we demand from the Father what we have no right to. We separate ourselves from communion with the Father. We squander the Father's gifts to us in a life of dissipation. And in our wretched desperation we realize that we do not deserve to be called the Father's son or daughter. We need this priceless knowledge of self just as the prodigal son needed his prolonged, anguish-filled retreat.

In other words, like the prodigal son we are "still a long way off." The knowledge of our sins can either condemn us or it can fill us with confidence to return to the house of the father. As mixed-up and twisted as the prodigal son is, some grace manages to set him on the path home.

The father's response to the sight of his sinful son contains nothing of the self-righteousness, the legalism, the vengefulness, or the vindictiveness found in the hearts of the Pharisees and scribes. Rather, the overwhelming compassion of the father appears in a threefold action: He runs to his son, he falls on his son's neck in an embrace, and he kisses him.

The running signifies the unabated initiative of the Father to be reconciled with his wayward children at all costs. The embrace signifies the Father's desire to have us back, not as dutiful slaves, but as partakers of his boundless love. And the kiss communicates to us a sharing in the Father's own life and being, like the breath of life God once breathed into Adam.

We cannot truly understand God the Father unless we put ourselves in the position of the prodigal son, receiving the Father's prodigal, unmerited love. Unfortunately, the other older son prefers to perceive himself as a slave: "All these years I served you." How perversely a warped reliance on worldly justice keeps us a long way off from the Father and seeks to abolish the very properties that are unique to his Fatherhood. Such is the state of the malicious Pharisees and scribes.

For the perfection of God the Father consists in giving himself wholly. As the father says to the older son, "Everything I have is yours." Yet that is precisely what the caustic, reproachful child has forgotten in his blasphemous attempt to make the good father look like a bad father. We cannot know the Father (we cannot even know ourselves!) unless we are willing to see ourselves in the prodigal son. Jesus eats with sinners to instill us with that piety that leads us away from dinner with the pigs and back to the house of the Father. And for this, we *must* celebrate and rejoice.

FIFTH SUNDAY OF LENT

DELEGATION OF GRACE
John 8:1-11

The scribes and the Pharisees capitalize on the guilt of a sinful woman in order to engineer a dirty trick far more reprehensible than her sin of adultery. One can assume that the woman's sin was a misguided search for love. But these manipulative men are brimming with hate. Deeply steeped in treachery, they expect Jesus to be a man just like them. Thus, they attempt to frame Jesus, contriving this false test in order to expose a double standard they hope to find in Christ. They sniff for some whiff of dissent in him. For the unveiling of hypocrisy in Jesus would validate the perfidy of these and all evil men. They want to reduce Jesus to their own rank pettiness.

However, the Son was not sent to condemn (Jn 3:17-18). Rather, condemnation is a fate we incur on ourselves because of our refusal to accept the Truth of Jesus (Jn 12:47). If we insist on belonging to what is below, like the scribes and Pharisees, we will die in our sins (Jn 8:24).

Sadly, sin seriously impairs the human ability to reason. And these opprobrious men get it wrong from the get-go. They drag the woman before Jesus because they presume that adultery is the worst sin that Christ can pronounce on. But the reality is that their presumption itself is a far worse sin than the weakness they damn in others. Presumption is considerably higher up in the catalogue of grave sins, second only to despair. For presumption negates any acknowledgment of the horror of our own sinfulness while holding fast to a delusional, self-accommodating notion of the working of divine justice and mercy.

How much we need the recollection and rectitude of Jesus Christ when confronted with conniving, adversity, and dissimulation — especially within ourselves. Yet, it is as impossible to find infallible integrity within ourselves as it is to find a lack of integrity in Jesus. This is the justice of heaven that completely eludes the scribes and Pharisees. Jesus longs to make us worthy of God through a merciful act of love. Heavenly justice must be given to us by Jesus. And Jesus gives it happily.

63

Christ says to the woman, "From now on do not sin any more." These words are not an ultimatum but rather an authorization. Christ invests the woman with supernatural assistance and delegates to her the grace to live habitually in freedom from sin. The Lord thereby redeems her from the slavery to sin (Jn 8:34). The Lamb of God who takes away the sin of the world (Jn 1:29) earlier issued a similar commission to the healed lame man (Jn 5:14). At his Resurrection, Christ will confer this power to save others from their sins on his apostles (Jn 20:23).

In short, the woman has been so overwhelmed by the love of Jesus that the future prospect of sin remains forever repulsive. What she had been seeking faultily in sex she has found in the chaste love of Jesus Christ.

The fact is that it is not so much our sin but rather the way that we respond to it that gives us the big picture of our moral condition. The guilt-ridden accusers skulk away in their shame like Judas from the Last Supper table (Jn 13:30). But the woman stays with Jesus without a word of denial or protestation on her lips about her sin. She is left alone with Jesus like one in love with God in adoration before the Blessed Sacrament. Jesus is left alone with us to remind us of his mercy.

Passion Sunday

Braced for Betrayal
Luke 22:14 — 23:56

Jesus enters into Jerusalem to confer on us a Kingdom. To receive this Kingdom we must enter into the new covenant Christ makes in his Blood. And yet, the first assertion Jesus makes after his Words over the cup is that he will be betrayed. The betrayal begins in the apostles' bickering about which of them is the greatest. But the kingship of Christ's Kingdom has nothing to do with lording one's authority over others. Rather, it is about remaining little. Whenever we neglect Christ's command to serve, the lure of betrayal begins braying in our ear. Therefore, this Holy Week calls us to be attentive to the subtle yet insidious ways that we betray Jesus in our words and actions.

We must never forget how much our communion with Christ changes and identifies us. Peter learns this the hard way by the fire. The arrest of Jesus calls his whole commitment to Christ into doubt. But seemingly all the world knows Peter to be "one of them." Peter's fidelity to Jesus has impressed even the faithless. Yet, it is that very oneness with Christ that Peter now attempts to deny. However, it is too late; Peter cannot return to the exemption of anonymity, to the immunity of the unrenowned. Since Peter has heard Jesus, Peter is not unheard-of. Anymore, to deny Jesus is to deny himself.

The world aches to make us squeamish about our commitment to Jesus Christ. Notice that the dialogue by the fire never bothers to raise a single question about what Peter believes. No theological debate ensues. Instead, it is enough that Peter has shared the company of Jesus Christ. Peter stands out simply because he was with Jesus. Thus, Christians are called to be outstanding in those controversial, inconvenient situations of the world that make us squirm. Because of our conformity to Christ, we Christians must remain conspicuous in our convictions when confronting others too eager to forswear their responsibilities.

To deny knowing Jesus is one thing. To deny that Jesus is King is another. Yet, the whole assembly before Pilate charges Christ with presuming a kingship that is not his. For if Christ is the King of the Jews, then the people must give some explanation of why they refuse to be subject to him. But there is no good reason for failing to reverence Christ as King. Therefore, they must contrive to discredit his kingship. In order to live unfettered in the slavery of sin, the people must kill the King.

We are guilty of a similar betrayal any time we opt for opinions or points of view that dissent from the Truth of Christ. Every willful imposition of our own self-serving outlook remains an attempt to kill Christ the King. Who needs him when *we* are gloriously reigning?

Yet, the good thief sees beyond the cowardice and ruthlessness of the world. Perhaps something about his own poor choices, resulting now in utter powerlessness, makes him especially sensitive to the kingship of Christ. More than that, the good thief recognizes the unique kind of King Jesus is: One who serves. And so, unlike the contemptuous crowds that demand Jesus to prove his kingship by saving himself (an act that would only betray his kingship), the good thief offers Christ the King the chance to serve. "Remember me when you come into your kingdom." The paradise of heaven is promised him because he has renounced the false paradise of the world.

The world can kill Jesus the King, but the new covenant of Christ will never die. To this, Joseph of Arimathea testifies as he approaches Pilate to ask for the body of Jesus. Joseph "was awaiting the kingdom of God." The hope he places in the Body of Christ assures us that the death of Jesus is not too late for us to repent of our betrayals. It is not too late to be counted among those who stand by Jesus in his trials.

EASTER SUNDAY

RESURRECTION AND REMEMBRANCE
Luke 24:1-12

The two men in dazzling garments who appear to the women at the tomb issue a command: "Remember." Notice that the angels do not resort to any extraordinary show of supernatural might in order to convince the women to believe in the Resurrection. Their resplendent demeanor hearkens back to Christ's Transfiguration, where he spoke of the Paschal Mystery with Moses and Elijah (Lk 9:29-31). This hints that there is something of a transfiguring encounter taking place here at the empty tomb — a transfiguration from within. It is not so much the presence of the angels as it is the testimony of the women's own memories that convinces them that Christ's Resurrection is real. The transfiguration of memory is necessary to be witness to the Resurrection, for the risen Christ is not seen by all, but only by those who believe (Acts 10:40-41).

Amazingly, the angels offer no new revelation. They simply encourage the women to recall what Christ has already said to them (Lk 9:22, 44). For Christ's saving Words, that will not pass away (Lk 21:33), continue to exercise their power on all who live in recollection. "And they remembered his words." The Blessed Virgin Mary sings of the mindfulness of God regarding the offer of his mercy (Lk 1:54). Zechariah praises God for remembering his holy covenant (Lk 1:72). This encounter at the tomb is God's Easter invitation to share in his own mindfulness.

The key to this redemptive remembrance is found in what the women seek: The Body of the Lord Jesus. For Christ's Body remains the means for connecting with Christ's Words and deeds. At the Last Supper, as Jesus takes the bread, he says: "Do this in memory of me" (Lk 22:19). Coming with their jars of spices, the women assume that the lifeless body of Jesus will be the only remaining link to the love they once shared with him. But as they remember Christ's Words, their faith is awakened.

Without the Eucharist, our memories of the Paschal Mystery would fade and decompose like a corpse in a tomb. Without the living Body of Christ we would lapse into apathy and neglect. As the women come to the tomb seeking a cadaver, they remember how to remember. The sacrifice of the Eucharist is a real, unique event of history that does not pass away. The event of the cross and Resurrection transcends all times, abiding and drawing all people out of the darkness of the tomb and into the daybreak of the Resurrection. We are to remember by entering into that saving sacrifice as fully as the women entered the tomb.

The power of the remembered Words of Christ appears in the way that they affect the apostle Peter. To the other apostles, the women's story of the encounter with the angels seems like nonsense. But Peter listens, considers, and then gets up. This "getting up" is itself a resurrectional verb. It recalls the moment that Mary rose and preceded in haste to make her Visitation to Elizabeth: A meeting in which the Word in her womb transformed Elizabeth and the son in her womb, John the Baptist. It mimics as well the prodigal son when he rises up and returns to his father, where he expects to be received back as a slave. But the Word of love spoken by the father transforms his desolation as it reinstates him as a true son.

Jesus Christ has risen! We rise with him — to remember and to be amazed.

Second Sunday of Easter

Always in Our Midst
John 20:19-31

"Jesus came and stood in their midst." The Word, who from the beginning was in God's presence, is forever in our midst. But as the prologue of the Gospel of John cautions us: "The Word became flesh and made his dwelling among us. . . . He came to what was his own, but his own people did not accept him" (Jn 1:14, 11). We manage to find so many ways to resist Jesus in our midst. A number of them are at work today: Darkness, hiding, locked doors, fear, skepticism, obstinacy. Easter is about the full acceptance of the Person of Jesus Christ always in our midst, risen to raise us up from all our deadly resistance.

Thus, carrying on from Christmas, Christ once again comes to his own. "[He] stood in their midst." The posture of Christ is not an immaterial detail. Rather, it is a theological assertion. This action recalls and fulfills the testimony of John the Baptist: "There is one among you one whom you do not recognize . . . whose sandal strap I am not worthy to untie" (Jn 1:26-27). On the last day of the festival in Jerusalem, Jesus stands up in the temple and cries out: "Let anyone who thirsts come to me and drink" (Jn 7:37). Mary Magdalene at the tomb catches sight of the risen Jesus standing (Jn 20:14). And the risen Christ stands on the seashore calling to his disciples, his "children," beckoning them to breakfast. In other words, the standing of Jesus in our midst summons us to the humility needed to recognize and respond to his presence. He stands to speak to the deepest yearnings and longings of our soul. He stands to rescue us from our sorrow and to instill us with the Father's love. He stands to call us to himself and to impart to us a sharing in his risen life.

Like that great moment in creation when God breathed life into Adam, the New Adam now comes to his disciples and, in an act of re-creation, breathes on them. When God first breathed, mere matter became a man. Now, however, when the risen Jesus breathes on his disciples, they become like God: They possess the divine power to forgive sins. The first man and woman rebelled in disobedience and forfeited their relationship with God in their futile attempt to become divine. Today God himself comes to those who are least deserving, those desirous only of being forgotten, and freely gives them his divinity. When Jesus is in our midst we become like him.

The deadly sin of Adam and Eve drove them to hide from God in their nakedness. The risen Jesus comes to where the disciples are hiding to free them from their sin-driven fear. To do so, in a way Jesus himself becomes naked. He shows them his brutalized body, and, later, he commands Thomas to touch his ever-present wounds. We must believe that the friendship lost by Adam and Eve has now been restored by the death and Resurrection of Christ. That is what Jesus declares when he says, "Peace." Love is real — yet no one has ever seen it. Blessed are those who have not seen and have believed.

In turn, the disciples of Jesus must be seen. We are called to bear the marks of Christ's crucifixion in our own bodies as a means of touching others so as to bring them to faith. All must believe that Jesus Christ is the "Son of God." Sometimes it takes the experience of unbearable woundedness or grievous loss, like the woman at the well (Jn 4:25) or Martha at the death of Lazarus (Jn 11:27), to come to confess that truth.

From now on, every day is Easter; always Jesus comes and stands in our midst to give us life in his name, life to the full (Jn 10:10).

THIRD SUNDAY OF EASTER

"DO YOU LOVE ME?"
John 21:1-19

Many of us have had the sorrowful experience of losing a loved one before we could express our heartfelt love and say good-bye. But how many of us have had someone come back from the dead to ask us if we loved him? That is what happens to the apostle Peter today.

What prompts this question on the part of the risen Christ? Clearly, it has nothing to do with ego-fulfillment or merely settling an old score. In fact, Jesus asks about Peter's love, not for his own benefit, but for the apostle's. For in the previous two Resurrection appearances, nothing has been said about Peter's denial of Jesus at the fire. The Lord's inquiry gives Peter a chance to undo the damage he did through his denials. The questions enable Peter to take responsibility for his life and to put Jesus Christ at the center of it. For Jesus knows that if Peter were to decline total love of Christ, he would become a spectacular, stupefying failure. And so it is with us. Undoing his denials of Jesus Christ saves Peter from personal undoing.

But what does it mean to love Jesus? In the first posing of the question, Christ asks, "Do you love me *more than these?*" True love of Jesus surpasses every other love of our life. The Lord earlier warned that the man who loves his life will lose it (Jn 12:25). Thus, to love Jesus most means fostering a holy self-forgetfulness in which we remain willing even to lose our life. Conversely, when we put ourselves first, we cannot get enough. We live self-obsessed, in constant suspicion, insecurity, and defensiveness. Peter's fireside interrogation (Jn 18:15-18, 25-27) demonstrates how futile and destructive that proves to be. To love Jesus more than all else means to lay down our life for our Friend, Jesus (Jn 15:13). Only by espousing Christ as the all-embracing Reality of our life do we reverse the self-induced threat of potential ruin.

Yet, Jesus asks Peter a second time, "Do you love me?" The repeated query indicates that Peter has not answered satisfactorily the first time. In fact, some of the truest professions of love begin with the words, "I'm

71

sorry." The truth is, Peter *cannot* love Jesus completely until he has been purified and consumed by God's love. The Eucharistic circumstances of the present encounter underscore this.

Perhaps that is why the Lord addresses Peter as "Simon, son of John." In referring to Peter's birth name and biological father, Jesus indicates how much Peter needs to be regenerated in the Father's love in order to love Jesus worthily and wholly. If we are not possessed of this ever-generating love of the Father, then we cannot love Christ (Jn 8:42). To love Jesus means to accept God the Father as our own, for we need to be generated in the Father's love at every moment. That is, we need to be in a living, dynamic union with the Father at every instant. In that union we realize who we are, where we come from, and how to live only for God. To do so means believing in Jesus as the Son (Jn 16:27) and rejoicing to have Jesus return to the Father (Jn 14:28). Thereby our ability to receive the Father's love and to love Jesus in return will be perfected.

And finally, true love of Jesus is evidenced in loving actions: "Feed my sheep." Anyone who loves Jesus is true to his Word (Jn 14:23). Anyone who loves Jesus obeys his commandments (Jn 14:21). Christ's love is not meant to be rulish but liberating. Every act changes us. Every act performed in conformity and out of obedience to Jesus Christ leads us away from the damning patterns of our past life and ushers us surely into the embrace of the Good Shepherd. We know that we love Jesus thoroughly when that is what we ourselves become.

Fourth Sunday of Easter

Good Shepherding
John 10:27-30

Sheep are usually kept either to be eaten or turned into sweaters. But Jesus has something revolutionary in mind for us his sheep. Unlike those raised to become lamb chops, the Good Shepherd destines us to have eternal life. However, eternal life does not mean simply living forever; rather, eternal life is to know the Father and the one whom he has sent, Jesus Christ (Jn 17:3).

There is a special connection — a rapport — between this Gospel passage and John 3:16: "For God so loved the world that he gave his only Son, that everyone who believes in him might not perish but might have eternal life." In giving us his Son, the Father has given us to his Son as sheep. In other words, it is the destiny of Jesus Christ to honor the Father by shepherding us who would otherwise remain unenlightened, wayward, and prey to disaster. In the exercise of this tender, extravagant care, Jesus reveals that the Father and he are one. The special dynamic between of the Good Shepherd and the sheep makes comprehensible for us the otherwise unfathomable communion of Father and Son.

It is absolutely imperative that the sheep remain in the shepherd's hand and in the hand of the Father. Out of love, the Father has entrusted everything into the Son's hand (Jn 3:35). In rebellion, sinful people try to get their hands on Jesus (Jn 10:39). The knowledge that the Father has handed everything over to Jesus makes him want to serve his subjects in even the most menial way (Jn 13:3). In order to enter into the oneness of the Father and the Son, it is not enough for our concept of sheep-hood to change; so must our concept of the Shepherd.

Perhaps we do not sufficiently appreciate the horror of "perishing," most compellingly illustrated in the example of Judas (Jn 17:12). Perishing is the inevitable outcome of things limited to the natural (Jn 6:12, 27). Sheep without a shepherd are left with only their natural instinct to survive. But even that cannot be trusted. In the same way, it is only to the degree that we allow ourselves to be shepherded by Christ that eternal life becomes ours. For the one who loves his own natural life perishes (Jn 12:25). But the one who spurns worldly living receives the Good Shepherd's supernatural ability to know, love, and respond to God. For the greatest fear the grips that heart of Jesus as he approaches his Passion is the prospect of one of the Father's sheep perishing (Jn 18:9).

By accepting the shepherding of the Son we come to recognize the Father's incomparable greatness. Those who reject the good shepherd disdain the greatness of the Father (Jn 4:12; 8:53). For the greatness of the Father appears in the works he has given his Son to do. Yet, as great as Jesus works are, those who allow themselves to be shepherded will see even greater ones (Jn 1:50; 5:20) and will actually perform them (Jn 14:12). The greatness of the Father is to be our greatness.

The key to all this is hearing and heeding the Shepherd's voice. The good sheep is like the devoted best man who listens for the groom's voice in order experience the humble joy it gives (Jn 3:29). The voice that Jesus offers to obedient sheep will one day speak to draw forth the dead from their tombs (Jn 5:25, 28). In short, to be a good sheep means reverencing the reason for the Incarnation: "For this reason I was born . . . to testify to the truth. Everyone who belongs to the truth listens to my voice" (Jn 18:37).

Fifth Sunday of Easter

Loving With the Love of Jesus
John 13:31-33a, 34-35

Before his death, Jesus gives us a new commandment: We are to love one another as he has loved us. The clue to that love appears in what he calls us: "Children." Jesus has loved us with the Father's love. The transforming power of that love in turn makes us the Father's children as well. More exactly, Jesus loves us *as* he loves his Father, for we are the Father's gift to Jesus. As a good Son, Jesus loves everything that the Father has given him. And we are chief among those gifts. Jesus calls us children so that we *can* love one another as he has loved us. Whenever we love others, it is because Jesus loves in us and through us; we love others with Jesus' own love.

The ability to love unfailingly with the very efficacy of Christ remains the fulfillment of one of the first promises in the Gospel of John: "To those who did accept him he gave the power to become children of God" (Jn 1:12). Christ makes clear that authentic childhood depends on more than established ancestry: "If you were Abraham's children, you would be doing the works of Abraham" (Jn 8:39). The ability to follow Christ's example of love is precisely what Jesus mediates to us as children of the Father. The greatest example remains that of Christ's death whereby he gathered into one all the dispersed children of God (Jn 11:52). That gathering begins as soon as Jesus is raised from the dead when he calls to his disciples on the sea: "Children. . ." (Jn 21:5).

The moment we relinquish this gift of spiritual childhood then a lesser *modus vivendi* takes over in our life. For the key to childhood is dependency. Every other relationship is predicated on equality. To disregard spiritual childhood is to posit a parity with God that is nothing less than delusional. Only God can make us his equal, and he does so through spiritual childhood that treasures divine charity above every other motivation, attitude, and behavior. We cannot glorify God if jealousy, anger, spitefulness, selfishness, greed, sensuality, pride, or any other principle rules our life. Remember that the backdrop for this whole discussion is the example of the one who betrayed the love of Jesus: Judas.

Thus, Jesus communicates this supreme truth via a commandment. The command to love is not a good idea or a useful suggestion: It is divine Revelation. The command is not even of Jesus' own making; he has received it from his Father (Jn 10:18; 12:49; 14:31). It reveals something about ourselves that we could never discover without Jesus Christ. Left to ourselves, we would be inclined to believe that there is no way out of the pettiness, bitterness, resentment, cruelty, etc., that plagues our life. This commandment springs the door of that insidious trap.

The possession of this new commandment keeps us from giving into our own impaired judgment and self-centered ideas. It guarantees a certain objectivity in Gospel-living. And to insure that we are not kidding ourselves about our love of Jesus and others, the Lord makes the keeping of his commandments key to that love (Jn 14:15, 21; 15:10, 14). In this way, we, like Jesus, glorify God by manifesting and communicating the very goodness of God in the integrity and the vivacity of our Christian life.

Sixth Sunday of Easter

Home, Remembrance, and Peace
John 14:23-29

The Lord Jesus accommodates our skepticism, reticence, and doubtfulness by telling us three important things before his death so that we will believe them when they come to pass.

Christ first promises that the Father and he will come and make their dwelling with the believer who loves Jesus by keeping his Word. The pledge seems somewhat absurd, for why would the immaterial, all-powerful God require a place to dwell? Long ago, when the Ark of the Covenant was being kept in a tent and King David was living in a royal palace, David got the idea to build a temple for God. But the Lord said to him: "I have not dwelt in a house from the day on which I led the Israelites out of Egypt to the present. . . . The LORD . . . will establish a house for you" (2 Sm 7:6, 11). Therefore, although God does not require a place or a space to live, the Lord longs to dwell in the hearts of the just — a righteousness offered in the Word.

The home is where we experience the love of father and mother, and where we learn to respond to that love in obedience. The home is where we realize that we are loved — a lessen crucial to our growth, maturity, responsibility, and self-possession. The home is where we develop our abilities, realize our powers, and find ourselves. The home is where we are most secure, most relaxed, most ourselves. God promises to make his home within us so that we can come into our own and be "at home" with God.

The problem is that sin works to exclude us from our true homeland, heaven. However, that conversion of heart that keeps us obedient and devoted to Christ's Word gives us access to heaven. And we need not wait until death to enjoy it. Jesus Christ has reconciled heaven and earth in himself. When we pray, "Our Father, who art in heaven," we are proclaiming that God's majesty and presence are even now dwelling in the hearts of the just.

77

How wonderful this blessed reciprocity: Jesus dwells in us the more we make our home in him (Jn 15:4) by living out of his Word in all its fullness. As we establish ourselves in the Blessed Trinity, God makes our soul his heaven where we live with him, ever docile, vigilant to his creative action, faithfully adoring. God dwells in us to divinize us and to make us instruments of divinization.

In his preaching, Jesus once promised that all shall be taught by God (Jn 6:45) — a promise to be fulfilled in the sending of the Holy Spirit. Even more, the Holy Spirit will remind us of all that Christ has told us. The act of remembering is a crucial aspect of spiritual growth in the Gospel of John. The disciples understand the real significance of Christ's cleansing of the temple as they recall key words of Scripture (Jn 2:17). After the Resurrection, the disciples recall Christ's prophecy about destroying and raising up the temple (Jn 2:22). In the same way, after Christ's glorification recollection makes them understand the true significance of his triumphal entry into Jerusalem (Jn 12:16). We need the supernatural agency of the Holy Spirit to remind us of the truth. Without him, our natural, fallible minds soon forget everything that matters most in life.

And Jesus bestows upon us peace. This is the first time we hear this Word on the lips of Jesus in the Gospel of John, but it will become one of the most important words in the Resurrection appearances (Jn 20:19, 21, 26). Peace is that divine gift that enables us to live in friendship with God in tranquility, rectitude, and confidence. Christ commands us to do what is humanly impossible: Not to be afraid, and to rejoice in the face of horror. Peace empowers us to do both.

Seventh Sunday of Easter

FATHER
John 17:20-26

Christ's priestly prayer is not just for his priests but also for those to whom they will minister, especially via their preaching. The Lord's prayer addressed to the Father helps us to understand why priests are called "Father," for his prayer forms them for the task of generating believers who will be one as the Father and the Son are one. It manifests how God the Father is to be preached.

A good father loves us simply because we are his. Jesus reveals the consummate goodness of God the Father by making known the Father's name to us. The Father's name becomes our very identity, our heritage, our means of belonging. The gift of the Father's name proclaims that we do not belong to ourselves but to the Father. Thus, the Father deeply esteems each child, not because of the great things we may do, but simply because we are his.

The shocking truth of it all is that the Father loves us even as he loves Jesus. And he desires that love to remain active in us. Too often we dismiss the Father as some cosmic noble Soul who puts up with us out of pity. We mistakenly reduce God's love to an act of humoring, of mere toleration motivated by obligation instead of heartfelt affection. We think of the Father as some overindulgent uncle who forbears with our folly when in fact he would prefer to be doing something else. He endures our antics without complaining, but cringing all the while. However, the moment that the Father stops loving us is the moment when the Blessed Trinity would end. It simply is not possible. For this reason, Jesus wants us with him where he is. We remain eternally part of the way that the Father loves the Son.

Moreover, a good father knows the very worst things about us, and yet he loves us even more in that knowledge precisely because we need to be loved. A good father does not get upset with our failures, but rather blesses us with the mercy that enables us to rise above them. Fathers know that there is nothing innately "righteous" about their children. In fact, the most excellent love that we can show to our father is a love devoid of all self righteousness. Thus, Jesus addresses his Father as "Righteous," for the Father alone possesses the power to make others good and worthy of union with himself. God the Father purifies and justifies us through an act of love whereby we can finally give to God the allegiance and worship that he deserves as God. When we love the Father as Righteous he lifts us beyond ourselves to him.

And finally, a good father believes his child can do anything that the father wishes because he wants only what the child *can do*. Jesus gives us the Father's own glory so that we will be brought to perfection. How readily we dismiss "perfection" as some far-reaching ideal impossible to achieve. And so it is — unless it is given to us from on high (Jn 3:27). For true perfection is not about doing everything flawlessly. Authentic perfection means fulfilling the end predestined for us by God. Jesus' God-given vocation was to lay down his life out of love for the Father in order to save the world. Thus Christ showed his love for his disciples to the end, that is, he showed them how perfect his love for his Father was before he died (Jn 13:1). The key to perfection entails doing what the Father wants us to do and enables us to do. That is why Jesus gives us the Father's glory — a sharing in the very goodness of God that empowers us to do whatever the Father wills. Therein lies our happiness, our fulfillment, our peace.

Pentecost Sunday

Holy as the Spirit
John 14:15-16, 23b-26

At first glance, we might surmise that Jesus is stipulating an ultimatum today: "If you love me, you will keep my commandments." But there is nothing of a "do this or else" mentality about these words. Rather, Christ's declaration stands as supreme consolation: We *can* keep the Lord's commandments because we live in his love; in fact, keeping his commandments constitutes the lover's deepest desire. The question is, How do we keep that love alive? That is what the gift of the Holy Spirit on Pentecost is all about.

So often the reality of the Resurrection appears in the quality of our reactions to things. Either our reactions are authentically spiritual, i.e., informed by divine charity, or they are carnal, i.e., motivated by vicious motives like spite, self-seeking, sensuality, jealousy, pride, etc. Life confronts us with ongoing conflict and combat. We wake each day to face the daily rebellion within. What will win out: Death or Resurrection? If Jesus Christ remains the greatest priority of our life, then the Lord promises us a divine Advocate to aid us in our struggle. The desire for nothing less than Gospel love disposes us to receive the Holy Spirit. The venal, on the other hand, regard the Holy Spirit in vain.

How does the Holy Spirit keep us loving and obedient to Christ's commandments? First, he teaches us the truth about ourselves that without the Spirit's insight would terrify us. The Holy Spirit instructs us in everything (Jn 14:26), especially about how to understand and respond to sin in our life. He guides us from the truth of self-knowledge to the merciful truth of redemption (Jn 16:13).

Second, the Holy Spirit reminds us of all that Christ has told us. More specifically, the memorializing of the Holy Spirit re-presents the saving events always active in the Words of Jesus Christ by applying them to our life here and now. Thus, Christ's offer of the Spirit geared to satisfying our deepest thirst (Jn 7:37-39) renews itself from one moment to the next in the outpouring of Pentecost. In a very special way, the Holy

Spirit reminds us of Christ's Words of forgiveness every time we approach the sacrament of penance (Jn 20:22-23).

And finally, the Holy Spirit is with us always. John the Baptist recognized the pertinacity of the Spirit when he first set eyes on Jesus (Jn 1:32). Just as the Baptist saw the Spirit in Christ, so we can see the Holy Spirit in ourselves as we pray for him to raise us above our sinful passions. For the presence of the Holy Spirit continues to beget us (Jn 3:5), transforming and converting our fleshly, worldly ways into spiritual ones.

But how easily people tend to forget the invisible, self-effacing Spirit. It prompts us, those privileged to receive the Holy Spirit who comes on Pentecost from the Father and the Son, to go forth in kind to bear witness on Christ's behalf (Jn 15:26-27). The grace of Pentecost calls us to be the Holy Spirit to others.

Holy Trinity Sunday

The Trinity's Innermost Secret
John 16:12-15

Just what is the "much more" that Jesus wants to tell us, and why cannot we "bear it now?" The Lord is concerned that if he tells us what fills his heart before we are disposed to receive it well, we may take it wrong. This same verb, "to bear, to carry, to take" appears several times in the Gospel of John. It relates how the crowd took up rocks to stone Jesus (Jn 10:31). Judas took hold of the purse reserved for the poor (Jn 12:6). This expression is used for Christ's carrying of the cross (Jn 19:17). And it describes how Mary Magdalene wants to take away Jesus' body which she believes the gardener has moved (Jn 20:15).

In other words, the crowd takes up stones because they cannot bear to hear Jesus declare that the Father and he are one. The embezzling Judas cannot bear Christ's merciful welcome and words to the woman who lavishly anoints his feet. Because of her consuming sorrow, Mary Magdalene finds the words of the unrecognized risen Christ unbearable. In short, we can bear what Jesus longs to tell us to the extent that we relinquish our self-righteousness, our betrayal, and our doubt by staying united to the cross of Jesus. As we carry his cross we are carried away by his words and into the saving mystery of the Blessed Trinity.

To ready us for all Jesus wants to tell us, Christ informs us about the guidance of the Holy Spirit who "will speak what he hears." We do not often think about the Holy Spirit speaking — but in fact he does. In the Acts of the Apostles the Spirit tells Philip to catch up with the carriage of the Ethiopian eunuch (Acts 8:29). The Spirit tells Peter to go with the two men sent by Cornelius (Acts 10:19). The Holy Spirit tells the prophet and teachers assembled in Antioch to set apart Barnabas and Saul for his work (Acts 13:2). The Spirit admonishes Paul about future chains and hardship (Acts 20:23). And the Holy Spirit forewarns Paul about how his own people would bind him and hand him over to the Gentiles (Acts 21:11).

Thus, the Holy Spirit speaks to guide our witness to the faith, to

83

reveal God's will for us, to strengthen us in our vocation, to prepare us for suffering, and to fortify us to lay down our lives for love of God. Jesus understands that we cannot realize the full truth about ourselves until we accept the full truth about him from the Spirit of Truth. And the Truth of Christ is that he lives to die out of love for his Father in order to redeem sinners. We must seize this truth, not just with our minds, but with every act and intention of our lives. The Spirit comes to enable us to embrace Christ's Passion and to live ever united in his crucifying love.

Then, as the *Catechism of the Catholic Church* teaches us (221), we are ready to receive God's innermost secret. It is this: God himself is an eternal exchange of love, Father, Son, and Holy Spirit, and he destines us to share in that exchange. Christ longs for us to participate in the communion of the Blessed Trinity. That is what he has been waiting all his life to tell us.

Corpus Christi Sunday

Dismissing What Crowds
Luke 9:11b-17

The whole of Christ's earthly mission was ordered to reconciling everything in his Person, making peace through the shedding of his Blood, and uniting all people in the one love he shares eternally with the Father. Thus, the suggestion of the Twelve today nearly defies the very designs of divine Providence: "Dismiss the crowd." Christ has come, not to dismiss, but to convoke. The Kingdom of God that the Lord proclaims is itself a gathering of men and women around Jesus Christ whom the Father has raised up to share in his own divine life. To dismiss the crowd as the day draws to a close is to dispel the very ones whom Jesus has labored to draw close to himself.

The apostles are put off by the desert, for they see it as threatening wilderness devoid of shelter, sustenance, and security. Their limited human knowledge and experience begin to impinge upon their relationship with Jesus and the confidence they place in him. For they presume that God's all-powerful Providence cannot reach them in such a barren place. Yet, it was precisely in the desert that Jesus experienced Satan's temptations to reject the Father. And it was in the desert that the Father himself satisfied the hunger of his Son. Now, in this desert, Jesus demonstrates the Father's desire to feed all his children. The trick is not letting hunger, fear, or anxiety get the better of us.

For the desert offers definite advantages. In this lifeless place empty of diversion, amusement, and gratification we are all the more compelled to put our complete focus on the Body of Christ before us. For the characteristics of Jesus' human body express the divine Person of the Son of God. The apostles think that all they have are five loaves and two fish. In reality, in Jesus Christ, they have absolutely everything. Sometimes we need to be alone in a deserted place with Jesus Christ to realize in the depths of our soul that he is our everything.

Christ has come to supply every need. In Jesus, nothing is lacking and no one suffers want. All the Lord asks of the five thousand is what he asks of Christians each Sunday: To gather together as a sacred assembly, to unite in offering worship with Jesus the High Priest, to receive Holy Communion, and to go forth to share the remaining abundance with others yet unfed. After Mass is the time to go out to "the surrounding villages and farms."

The desert is also the place where the good shepherd goes in search of the single lost sheep (Lk 15:4). Thus, it is in the desert that the Twelve learn what it means to be shepherds of the Church. After the Resurrection, Jesus will say to Peter: "Feed my sheep" (Jn 21:17). But even now Jesus says to his apostles: "Give them some food yourselves." This great feast of the Body and Blood of Christ assures us that our relationship with the Lord Jesus makes of our life a kind of feast whereby we can feed others with the reconciliation, peace, and unifying love of God. Because of the Holy Eucharist, the desert has become a banquet table. Thanks to this sacramental repast — which itself means "thanksgiving" — hunger, fear, and anxiety are banished to the past. The Eucharist fills us with the might to dismiss anything that crowds out Jesus Christ from our life.

Tenth Sunday in Ordinary Time

What Matters to Jesus
Luke 7:11-17

What catches Jesus' attention, makes him stop in his tracks, and moves him to change his plans? When Jesus sees the widow of Nain who has lost her only child, Luke tells us "he was moved with pity." The emotional response of Christ to this heart-wrenching sight is identical to the pity that prompts the good Samaritan to assist the brutalized traveler on the road. The Lord's pity is the same as that of the father of the prodigal son as he runs with abandon to be reconciled to his child. The pity of Jesus Christ reaches out both to those who have been victimized by the world and to those who have wreaked disaster on themselves by their sinful choices. Jesus notices us in our powerlessness and misery, and he himself takes the initiative to transform it.

There are three parts to the transformation. First Jesus approaches the mother and says, "Do not weep" — the last thing we would probably ever say to a woman in such distress. Yet, Jesus' motive is merciful. He knows how inimical weeping can be to believing. Unrectified emotion can mitigate our faith. Jesus forbids any weeping that stands in the way of trust and belief (Lk 23:28). He only allows the weeping that effects conversion, as with the penitent woman who wipes Jesus' feet with her tears (Lk 7:38), and Peter after his denial (Lk 22:62). Jesus himself weeps over Jerusalem (Lk 19:41) precisely because its people refuse to shed tears of repentance.

Moreover, Jesus steps forward and touches the coffin. Redemption is the result of physical contact with Jesus Christ. The Lord's touching of the coffin serves as a kind of sacramental action. In fact, it risks creating a scene in the midst of the large distraught crowd to whom Jesus is apparently a perfect stranger. Even more, pious Jews would be appalled by the defiling act of coming into bodily contact with the dead. But Christ touches the dead man then, and he continues to touch what is dead in us now through the sacraments. Every experience of the sacraments puts us in direct, personal, physical contact with Christ's Passion and Resurrection. When we avail ourselves of his life-giving touch, we are transformed.

And finally, Jesus commands the young man to arise. Yet his restored life does not give him carte blanche to live as he will. For Jesus gives him to his mother. The Lord's action in Nain foreshadows what Jesus will do on Calvary when he gives his beloved disciple to his Mother. The Gospel of Luke begins with the Visitation of Mary to Elizabeth. Now "God has visited his people" in a new way — but it still involves a mother. The Blessed Virgin Mary has led us to Christ. Through the gift of Mary to us on the cross, Christ leads us back to his Mother. She remains integral to our transformation. United in faith with the Mother of God in the new life of the sacraments, we will know our time of visitation (Lk 19:42).

ELEVENTH SUNDAY IN ORDINARY TIME

CHRIST'S RESPONSE TO SIN
Luke 7:36-8:3

Who is worthy to touch Jesus Christ? The Pharisee who hosts a dinner for Jesus has a preconceived idea so rank that one can almost smell it. Indeed, the unnamed Pharisee never actually voices his contempt, but rather says it to himself. Nonetheless, Jesus knows what he is thinking; he has read the Pharisees' minds before (Lk 5:22). This time Christ takes the Pharisee to task by means of a simile. Instead of reproving him outright, the Lord employs an analogy so as to prompt the Pharisee to think for himself, to see the error of his prejudice, and to make a Gospel judgment about what transpires between the woman and Jesus.

In fact, there are at least three preconceptions that must be overcome: About sinfulness, about forgiveness, and about Jesus himself. The Pharisee facilely presumes that sins of the flesh are the most deadly. He considers the woman's condition irreversible and her presence as pollution. Yet his presumption and his despair about the offer of mercy on her behalf stand as far deadlier sins. What about the Pharisee makes him any worthier of such a dinner guest? His sense of self-righteousness rivals only the contemptuousness he shows in condemning the woman.

And yet, the only way that we can recognize sin clearly is through the knowledge Revelation gives of God. We are told that the woman "learned" that Jesus was at table. In a way, she embodies the very purpose of the Gospel of Luke: To enable all to learn the truth about Revelation (Lk 1:4). Like the crowds that learn where Jesus is and respond in faith (Lk 9:11), the woman attends the Lord in the hopes of partaking of his mercy. That is the only way to recognize sin and to rectify it.

To live forgiven means to love energetically without limit. The others at table say to themselves: "Who is this who even forgives sins?" Jesus has already answered this criticism in healing the paralyzed man (Lk 5:20-24). But the Pharisees have not listened or learned. Forgiveness will be central to the way Jesus will teach his disciples to pray (Lk 11:4), to Christians' daily dealings with others (Lk 17:3-4), to Christ's last wishes on the cross (Lk 23:34), and to the Resurrection preaching of the Eleven (Lk 24.17). Each of these acts is an exercise of charity. We must love the forgiveness that Jesus has given us in our unworthiness more than we love others' respect for us (Lk 11:43). Otherwise, we set up two masters for ourselves — God's mercy vs. our own self-importance — and we can serve only one (Lk 16:13). The tender expression of love, kissing Christ in others like the father kissing the prodigal son (Lk 15:20) and anointing him like the good Samaritan (Lk 10:34), reveals to all the world the Master whom we serve.

The Pharisee perceives of Jesus as a prophet who should know "what sort of woman this is." Yet, like his fellow Pharisees later in the Gospel, this Pharisee fails to recognize that the reign of God is already in his midst (Lk 17:21) in Jesus. For no one knows the Son except the Father (Lk 10:22). To know the Son — and to know what Jesus knows — requires possessing a healthy sense of sin whereby we approach the presence of Christ in humility and confidence to receive the forgiveness of the Father who is rich in mercy. Then when we encounter sin in our lives, our response will be that of Christ's.

Twelfth Sunday in Ordinary Time

How to Know the Messiah
Luke 9:18-24

We must keep in mind that what transpires today is the fruit of Jesus' prayer. It is as if the Father is saying to his Son: It is now time to tell them. The Gospel relates that "Jesus was praying in solitude." In the Transfiguration account, we read that "Jesus was found alone" after the voice spoke from heaven, "This is my chosen Son; listen to him" (Lk 9:35-36). This present exchange between Jesus and his disciples foreshadows the revelation to come in the Transfiguration.

However, before Jesus can reveal the truth of himself, he must correct his disciples' mistaken preconceptions. For the Lord knows that any time human beings experience something outside of themselves, it is always associated with the experience *of* themselves — every experience of something external is at the same time an experience of self. Thus, to know who Jesus is means to know more truthfully who we are.

The crowds have come to three erroneous conclusions: Jesus is John the Baptist, Elijah, or a prophet. The crowds think only in conventional, convenient categories. They approach Jesus' identity as a sort of riddle to decipher. They use themselves as the standard for their assessment, in effect remaking Jesus according to their own image.

The crowds presume Jesus is John the Baptist because he is an authoritative teacher who tells them what to do (Lk 3:10ff). Because of his charisma and commanding presence, the crowds take Jesus for Elijah, the man of God who would return at the end of time. However, Christ's conversation with Elijah during the Transfiguration (Lk 9:30) clearly distinguishes the two. And the witness of Jesus' great miracles and wonders leads the crowds to label Jesus a prophet (Lk 7:16, 39). Like them, it is so easy for us to get bogged down in worldly ways of making sense of things, thereby disregarding the divine.

Jesus' twice-posed question requires the disciples to go beyond familiar, easy criteria that relegate Jesus to being "a good person." For

Jesus is totally unlike anyone else. His identity — our identity — can be discerned only in a loving relationship with him.

How is it that Peter recognizes Christ? Perhaps it is due to the fact that, in all his many dealings with Jesus, Peter never observed Jesus commit a single sin. Most likely, Peter's own sinfulness remained quite predominated in his consciousness. Since their first encounter, Jesus has been Peter's Messiah (Lk 5:8). The uniqueness of Jesus regarding sin sensitizes Peter to Christ's divine origin and purpose. Not only is Jesus sinless — he is the Christ who alone can save Peter from his sinful self.

Why then does Jesus rebuke them? Christ issues similar rebukes to demons who attempt viciously to expose Jesus before his time (Lk 4:35, 41). He rebukes as well the fever in Peter's mother-in-law (Lk 4:39), the storm-causing wind (Lk 8:24), an unclean spirit (Lk 9:42), and the precipitous disciples (Lk 9:55). In short, Christ rebukes anything that impedes deeper faith and union with him in love.

To recognize Jesus as the Christ of God is like suddenly discovering that a cherished friend is in fact a luminary or a long-lost relative. That knowledge necessarily changes our relationship with the loved one. For just as our loving relationship reveals the Truth of Christ to us, so does the perfection of that relationship assure us a lasting place in that truth. Outside that covenant of charity, we cannot come to full knowledge of Christ, even if demons rage or Christ himself informs us (Lk 22:66-67). To know Christ is to do the Father's will just as Jesus does. It means letting Jesus be the Messiah of our life.

Thirteenth Sunday in Ordinary Time

Being Taken Up
Luke 9:51-62

During the Transfiguration account which precedes today's Gospel, Jesus' face changed in appearance (Lk 9:29), becoming refulgent with the glory of the Father. Now the days for Jesus to be taken up into heaven are fulfilled. Therefore, Jesus becomes "resolutely determined" to journey to Jerusalem — literally, he sets his face toward Jerusalem (Lk 9:53). The face that has radiated the glory of the Father now turns to Jerusalem to glorify the Father in the Son's Passion, death, and Resurrection.

From this moment on we will hear a number of recurring themes in the Gospel of Luke all ordered to purifying us and deepening our participation in the Paschal Mystery. As the encounter with the Samaritans illustrates, we need to be disposed to enter into this mystery. Neither the defiance of the Samaritans nor the vindictiveness of the disciples prepares us for Calvary. Rather, Jesus specifies three qualities of worthy discipleship.

"The Son of Man has nowhere to rest his head." Even nonrational animals have a place to call home — but not the disciples of Jesus, for they are "at home" with Christ himself. The Son cannot rest until he fulfills the will of his Father. He finds his rest in founding the Kingdom. Similarly, we must evict all temptations to take refuge in our own safety and security. United in Christ's unrelenting fervor, we take up residence in the communion of the Blessed Trinity. As the letter to the Hebrews reminds us, "Christ was faithful as a son placed over his house. We are his house, if [only] we hold fast to our confidence and pride in our hope" (Hb 3:6).

Moreover, disciples must "let the dead bury their dead." There will always be legitimate excuses for procrastinating, for rationalizing, and disqualifying ourselves from discipleship. In weeks to come, Jesus will say even more forcefully: "If anyone comes to me without *hating* his father and mother . . . he cannot be my disciple" (Lk 14:26 [emphasis added]). As St. Ambrose observes, discipleship demands the postponing of human things in favor of the divine. Anyone who attempts to divide his pursuits only dwindles his devotion. He who allots his cares delays his advance in holiness. Therefore, discipleship calls for full surrender to the Providence of God the Father who in turn provides for every human need.

And finally, disciples are to put their hands to the plow and not look back. Christ wants all of us: Our affections, our emotions, our passions. He knows our craving need to be loved, to belong, and he knows how attached we become to support systems that seem to us irreplaceable. Yet, Gospel discipleship requires total abandonment. As the experience in Jerusalem will soon prove, denial and betrayal come all too easily, even to committed disciples. Nostalgia and homesickness can slyly sabotage the most avowed believer. That is why blessedness belongs to the single-hearted.

Thus, to set our face toward Jerusalem with Jesus means making the Father the source and the goal of our love. When the Father sees such resolve on our faces, then he takes us up into his love with his Son — our fulfillment.

FOURTEENTH SUNDAY IN ORDINARY TIME

THE KINGDOM AT HAND
Luke 10:1-12, 17-20

Not long ago Jesus declared that anyone who wishes to be his follower must deny himself, take up his cross each day, and follow in his steps (Lk 9:23). Today with the appointment of the seventy-two, Christ puts that injunction into action. They are to go on their way carrying no money, luggage, or sandals, and without stopping for casual banter. Incredibly, in spite of all these stiff stipulations, the seventy-two still go! Why?

Christ relies on the witness of his disciples. They carry on in the sacred tradition of John the Baptist, the herald who prepared the people for the coming of Christ (Lk 3:2-14). At that time, John spoke of Christ as a farmer poised to gather the wheat into his granary (Lk 3:15-18). Today Jesus speaks of the abundant harvest and the need for laborers to assist the Master of the harvest.

Jesus sends them out like lambs among wolves. In the time of Noah, God certainly could have re-created the world from nothing as in the beginning. But instead he loaded the ark with pairs of all the animals. God depended on their fruitfulness to propagate his new covenant after the flood. In the same way, the Lord depends on the testimony of the seventy-two. Their faith and conviction will tame ravaging beasts.

The first words of the seventy-two — "Peace . . ." — echo the words of the host of angels to the shepherds (Lk 2:14), Christ's Words to the sinful woman (Lk 7:50), the Lord's Words to the woman with the hemorrhage (Lk 8:48), and the Words of the risen Christ to the Eleven (Lk 24:36). In this way, the greeting of the seventy-two heralds the offer of redemption, forgiveness, healing, and divine friendship. Their salutation is somewhat sacramental in effect as it represents the saving presence of Christ.

The seventy-two are to eat and drink what is set before them. Eating and drinking with others holds an important place in the ministry of Jesus. While dining at the house of Levi, Jesus reveals his purpose to save sinners (Lk 5:29-32). During the dinner at the house of a Pharisee, Jesus teaches about the connection between forgiveness and love (Lk 7:36-50), and about humility and selflessness (Lk 14:1-24). Christ manifests the depths of God's mercy by eating with sinners (Lk 15:2). Such table communion anticipates the eternal feast of the Kingdom (Lk 22:30). Therefore, the seventy-two are to eat what is set before them as a sign of God's Providence (Lk 12:22, 29). Their presence at table indicates the redemptive initiative, the compassion, the integrity, and the tenderness of Jesus Christ.

In the same way, they manifest the presence of Christ by curing the sick. Jesus has given them power to tread upon serpents and scorpions and the full force of the enemy. The disciples' willingness to engage the most desperate problems head-on wins many to the faith.

And finally, the disciples are to preach the Kingdom, even after towns reject them.

Returning to Jesus they rejoice, but not because they have triumphed over demons; that could lead to the most egregious spiritual pride. Rather, they rejoice because they have permitted themselves to be chosen and commissioned by God. They have trusted the Lord in living with risk and suffering rejection. They come back to Jesus Christ transformed. No longer do they live for themselves, but for God who keeps their names as his own in heaven.

Why did the pairs of the seventy-two go despite such harsh conditions? Because they had everything they needed — Jesus Christ in each other.

Fifteenth Sunday in Ordinary Time

To Be a Neighbor
Luke 10:25-37

Why was the reaction of the good Samaritan to the victim on the road so different from that of the priest or the Levite? Luke tells us that the Samaritan was "moved with compassion" at the sight of him. Literally it means he was moved to pity in his inner organs. The same verb is used in the canticle of Zechariah to refer to the tender compassion of our God (Lk 1:78). This is the viscerally-felt compassion that moves Jesus to restore the life of the widow's son (Lk 7:13), and that sets the father running to reconcile with his prodigal son (Lk 15:20). In both instances, it is the act of seeing one in dire straits that triggers such compassion.

Yet, the priest and Levite were most likely not hard-hearted fellows. Luke tells us that the robbers left the victim half-dead, and to the priest and Levite he probably seemed like a corpse. They may have presumed there was nothing more to be done for the man, and it made no sense to incur defilement by touching the cadaver of an enemy. Let the dead bury the dead.

But the good Samaritan — represented as one possessed of Gospel love — refuses to presume about the condition of the victim. Something enabled him to look beyond the semblance of death and to reach out with generous compassion. Very likely, the good Samaritan saw himself in the victim. Perhaps he too was once brutalized and left for dead.

The memory of that horror now becomes an instrument of grace. Jesus raises the widow's son because he feels for her plight. The father becomes filled with compassion because the prodigal son's pain is his own. Our living union with Jesus Christ lifts us beyond our fears and self-imposed limitations to raise up others whose life depends on our charity.

While it may sound impertinent, the scholar's question, "And who is my neighbor?" is valid given the fact that there are three terms for "neighbor" used in Luke. Two of them refer to relatives, friends, and people living in one's neighborhood (Lk 1:58, 65; 14:12; 15:6, 9). But the word for neighbor used here is very special. It is rooted in the dynamic of com-

97

ing near to another, of approaching and drawing close. The good Samaritan becomes a true neighbor the moment his compassion moves him to approach the victim. This approach imitates the approach of Jesus to the widow of Nain (Lk 7:13), and Joseph of Arimathea to Pilate (Lk 23:52) — both "neighborly" acts in the Gospel sense. Christian neighborliness does not refer to where one lives; it is revealed in the way one acts.

The action of the neighbor to the victim is manifold. He consoles, soothes, and heals. He lifts the victim out of harm's way and provides him shelter and care. But he does not subjugate the victim to himself. In handing the innkeeper the two silver coins (with the promise of more), he hands back to the victim his freedom — the chance to begin his life again. True neighbors do not seek to indenture others or to arrogate the subservience of others.

What the robbers did to the victim, the world will soon do to Jesus. It will strip him, beat him, and go off leaving him to die on the cross. Christ's neighbors at that moment are those who draw near to Calvary — "all his acquaintances . . . including the women who had followed him . . ." (Lk 23:49) — and ourselves, if we are not unwilling to face the horror of death.

SIXTEENTH SUNDAY IN ORDINARY TIME

HOLINESS AFOOT
Luke 10:38-42

Imagine the first moment Jesus set foot in the home of Martha and Mary. What awe they must have felt to welcome such an august guest. Were they stymied by the privilege of Christ's presence? If so, when did awe fade into familiarity? At what point did Mary's admiration of Jesus mature into authentic piety? And what made Martha's wonder turn into whining?

We know the adage about familiarity breeding contempt. But Christ's familiarity with us remains his invitation to ever-deepening intimacy. Contempt creeps in whenever we depreciate the significance of his presence while overestimating our feeble efforts. Like so many of us, Martha presumes that her activism actually pleases God. She labors under the delusion that she can do something worthy of God without God. She presupposes that the God of peace prefers believers beleaguered by frenzy. Yet, we so easily side with such a twisted picture.

However, Martha's anxiety is deadly — as deadly as the seed that gets choked by obsessive cares (Lk 8:14). Repeatedly, Christ's warns against worry. It cannot increase our life-span (Lk 12:25). Even the smallest things of life lie beyond our powers, no matter how much the pestering of anxiety tries to persuade us otherwise (Lk 12:26). That is why, in particular, we should not be concerned about what we are going to eat (Lk 12:22). Everything will be provided for us through Jesus Christ — even the words we need to defend ourselves before adversaries (Lk 12:11). Therefore, the most important duty of the disciple is to devote oneself to the Word.

That is what Mary does at the feet of Jesus. There she finds herself in good company. The sinful woman receives the gift of Christ's peace at his feet (Lk 7:38). The exorcised demoniac terrifies the crowd because of his contemplative posture at the feet of Jesus (Lk 8:35). Jairus seeks healing for his daughter at Jesus' feet (Lk 8:41). At the feet of Jesus the healed leper proclaims praise and thanks (Lk 17:16). And to convince the Eleven of his identity, the risen Christ shows them his feet (Lk 24:39). Staying at the feet of Jesus is not a waste of time. It is the source of reconciliation, liberation, deepened faith, healing, and resurrection.

Mary has chosen the better part. Her action recalls Christ's choosing of the Twelve (Lk 6:13). Mary's choosing makes her chosen, and God will do justice to his chosen (Lk 18:7). Because the better part she chooses is the goodness of God himself (Lk 18:7). It is his personal privilege and prerogative to fill the hungry with good things (Lk 1:53). Our job is to remain in contemplation at the feet of Jesus, choosing him as the better part. For then we obey the voice of the Father: "This is my chosen son; listen to him" (Lk 9:35).

Seventeenth Sunday in Ordinary Time

Persistence and Paternal Care
Luke 11:1-13

No one knows the Father but the Son (Lk 10:22). The disciples discern this as they observe Jesus praying. And they want to know the one who keeps their Lord so absorbed in prayer. They realize that there remains something more to their relationship with Jesus — something only Christ can reveal to them. As they watch Jesus pray, they recognize their own vital need to pray. They cannot know Jesus Christ completely until they pray like him — and with him.

However, no one could have expected what Jesus teaches them in response to their request. For it was unheard of in Jesus' time to address God personally as "Father." Such a thing would have been considered shocking and sacrilegious. Yet, since his childhood, Jesus has been busy about his Father's affairs (Lk 2:49). It was promised that John the Baptist would turn the hearts of children to their fathers (Lk 1:17). In an extraordinary way, in Christ's revelation that prophecy now comes true.

Just as Christ's whole life is focused on the Father, so too is Christian prayer. Jesus emphasizes two dynamics of prayer: Persistence and paternal care. We may wonder why Christ endorses the efficacy of persistence over the exigencies of friendship. And yet, there is a divine logic to his plan. True friends accommodate even the least requests of their friends — at times in a lavish, non-discriminating, no-questions-asked kind of way. Love wants to please the beloved. Yet to pray with persistence purifies the desires of our heart. It filters out mere impulse and caprice. Persistence blesses us with real certainty about what we want. We will persist in only those things that truly matter. A lack of persistence often betrays a lackadaisical spirit about our soul's longing. It is just this sort of persistence that returns the prodigal son to the arms of his father.

Thus, we must ask like the blind man whose petition the disciples tried to squelch (Lk 18:35-39). We must seek like the woman in search of her lost silver piece (Lk 15:8-10). In this regard, we imitate Jesus Christ himself who has come to seek out and save what was lost (Lk 19:10). And we must knock, for God will treat us like the servants responding to the knock of their master (Lk 12:36). By virtue of all these efforts we offer the Father the chance to manifest his paternal love and care. Conversely, the lack of persistent, faithful prayer renders our knocking useless (Lk 13:25).

It is the hallmark of the Father to be good to the wicked (Lk 6:35). Even on the natural plane, fathers cannot resist the entreaties of their children. God the Father gives us what is we ask, not because we are good, but because he is. What father would give his child a snake or a scorpion? Unfortunately, we hear of far worse fathers in the news. But God the Father gives his children power to tread on snakes and scorpions (Lk 10:19). In other words, to pray the way Jesus teaches us — to pray to the Father — invests us with the very authority of the Father. Thereby we can rise above our natural wickedness and be compassionate as the Father is (Lk 6:36).

The Father draws us into the fullness of love that he shares with his Son by giving us the Holy Spirit. Thus, when we pray the Our Father, we are transformed in holiness like John the Baptist (Lk 1:15), the blessed Virgin Mary (Lk 1:35), Elizabeth (Lk 1:41), Zechariah (Lk 1:67), and Simeon (Lk 2:25) — all of whom were filled with the Holy Spirit as a fruit of their prayer. In short, as we pray the Our Father, Jesus does not simply reveal the Father to us — in the Lord's Prayer he reveals us to ourselves.

EIGHTEENTH SUNDAY IN ORDINARY TIME

WHAT LIFE CONSISTS OF
Luke 12:13-21

"Who do people say that I am?" The people consider Jesus a teacher, a healer, a wonder-worker, a prophet. However, the "friend" in the Gospel today mistakes Christ for a kind of juridical arbitrator at his disposal to rectify controversies surrounding the family bequest.

How petty these trifling squabbles must have seemed to the one who had set his face toward Jerusalem to meet his Passion. Here the sublime meets the venal. For the man in the crowd is more concerned with money than with the bonds of family. Yet, Christ is prepared to lay down his very life in order to make us his brothers and sisters. The man gripes about being gypped out of his parental inheritance. His grousing makes him oblivious to Christ's desire to give all God's children a share in the heavenly Father's legacy. Self-interest has made the man mean-spirited and small. His day resounds with "my brother" instead of "Our Father."

As a result, Jesus warns the crowd to take care to guard against all greed. In this respect, they will be like the shepherds guarding their flocks (Lk 2:8), like the angels guarding the Son of God (Lk 4:10), and like the strong man guarding the valuables in his courtyard (Lk 11:21). Any negligence or compromise on our part regarding the lure of greed jeopardizes our relationship with Jesus Christ, the Father, and the offer of the Kingdom.

Put plainly, one's life does not consist of possessions. That is, one's life cannot be made secure by possessions. Jesus will reiterate this truth several times before his death. He will soon tell his disciples: "Sell your belongings and give alms" (Lk 12:33). And also: "Everyone of you who does not renounce all his possessions cannot be my disciple" (Lk 14:33).

The danger lies in amassing anything that gives us the impression of being "rich." The present parable about the rich man and his large barns serves as a prelude to the parable about the rich man and Lazarus (Lk 16:19ff). Being wealthy is deadly because of the attitudes attendant to it. Wealth often breeds a false sense of security and self-sufficiency. It poisons us into thinking we can get by without God. It infects us with a feeling of entitlement by which we believe that we have the right to special treatment — to be exempted, dispensed, and upgraded over the unwashed masses.

People in love with their money often exude a suffocating air of disdain and condescension. Privilege, superiority, and elitism become their blessed trinity. No wonder the rich man can expect difficulty trying to enter heaven (Lk 18:25). The wealthy become accustomed to getting things their own way. Yet, heaven refuses to yield to the tirades of the rich. Thus, for the unconverted rich person, the attempt to enter heaven is a kind of hell. To the rich man, heaven remains superfluous. Who wants to be there if we can't impose our own will?

Most likely, if the man in today's Gospel were not vexed by some self-centered need, he would have paid no attention to Jesus at all. Possessions and wealth make us equally forgetful and dismissive of God. For this reason, Jesus has commanded us to pray, "Give us this day our daily bread." Our daily asking keeps us from getting self-satisfied. And by asking only for bread, we stave off the gluttony of greed.

Thus, Christ asks us to live with uncertainty, contingency, and maybe even a little temporal injustice (Lk 6:27-30). All these things keep us poor. And poverty keeps us dependent upon God. And humble dependency upon God is the key to perfection. That is what matters to God. That is what life consists of.

Nineteenth Sunday in Ordinary Time

Entrusted and Trusting
Luke 12:32-48

There is a pronounced resonance between today's Gospel and the episode about the shepherds on Christmas Eve (Lk 2:8-18). The cue comes when Jesus refers to his disciples as "little flock." The setting for both accounts is night when thieves strike, lamps need to be lit, and the master appears in the second or third watch. In fact, the summons to vigilance is in fact a command to stay awake. The shepherds witness the glory of the Lord because they remain awake and watchful in the fields with their flocks. Peter sees the glory of Christ's transfiguration because he awakens (Lk 9:32). So too, to stave off the burgling of the thief, one needs to stay awake.

In the passage about the shepherds and this one, the people are instructed, "Do not be afraid." An angel delivers the same message to Zechariah (Lk 1:13) and the Blessed Virgin Mary (Lk 1:30). To this point, Jesus has issued this command to Simon Peter (Lk 5:10) and Jairus (Lk 8:50). In other words, fearless living remains a supernatural gift given by God to enable his chosen ones to live by faith in freedom. The good news that Jesus reveals today will culminate in the parable of the three servants and the sums of money. The third servant's downfall will come precisely because he refuses to live without fear (Lk 19:21) — he rebuffs what God makes possible to him.

For the Father has entrusted us with very much. It has pleased him to give us the Kingdom. The angels announce this same divine delight to the shepherds: "Peace to those with whom [God's] favor rests" (Lk 2:14). At Jesus' baptism the Father's voice declares: "You are my beloved Son; with you I am well-pleased" (Lk 3:22). What pleases the Father is to reveal the mysteries of heaven to the merest children (Lk 10:21). Thus, we please the Father when we use to his glory the great graces and abilities he has entrusted to us.

Notice that the fate of the servant who abuses his authority and power is to be cut off from the master and banished to dwell with the unfaithful. His guilt goes beyond even his appalling irresponsibility, abusiveness, and hedonism. Indeed, his most grave sin is a sin against faith. He betrays his covenant with his master. He co-opts the privileges of the master for his own private self-gratification. He shows himself to be a treacherous cad towards the master who entrusts him with so much.

To be assigned a place among the faithful means to light our lamps — literally, to keep them burning, like the hearts of the disciples on the road to Emmaus (Lk 24:32). At an hour they did not expect, the Son of Man came to them. Neither did the shepherds expect the coming of Christ at Christmas. But because they were docile, trusting, obedient, and devout, they were well-prepared for the mystery revealed to them. Just as they saw the Incarnate God lying in a manger, so will Christ's faithful disciples rejoice to recline at the table of the Eucharist with the Master.

Twentieth Sunday in Ordinary Time

On Fire
Luke 12:49-53

Fire terrifies and destroys. Fire warms and helps in generating life. Fire purifies and refines. Fire transforms. Jesus comes to set the earth on fire. He means for the blaze to do a little bit of each. The fire Jesus yearns to ignite is that of the Father's love in the hearts of those caught up in lesser things.

Jesus' wish fulfills John the Baptist's prophecy: "He will baptize you with the holy Spirit and fire" (Lk 3:16). When the Holy Spirit descends on the apostles and the Blessed Mother on Pentecost he does so in the form of tongues of fire signifying the transforming energy of the Holy Spirit. In this holocaust the Spirit communicates to us the supernatural life that originates in the Father.

However, before the blaze of Pentecost burns, Jesus must receive the baptism of his Passion. Until that moment, Christ feels anguish. Peter's mother-in-law experiences anguish until Jesus stands over her and addresses the burning fever (Lk 4:39). The entire population of the Gerasene territory suffers anguish over the plummeting of the herd of pigs into the lake (Lk 8:37). Anguish will characterize the nations of the earth at the second coming (Lk 21:25). In other words, anguish arises as a result of sickness, loss, and anxiety. And Jesus Christ is the only answer to it all.

But Christ has not come to endorse a deficient peace of our own making. Jesus has not come to sanction a self-styled status quo or to collude with our self-contentment. How often in our spiritual life do we conspire to make God complicit in our easy concessions and slipshod excuses? Unredeemed human nature so longs for the Lord to ratify its self-indulgent mediocrity — the good-enough-Catholic syndrome. However, Christ burns with anguish until every trace of compromise, complacency, laxness, dissent, and mollycoddle Christianity is purged from the earth. Sadly, that is what the rich man too late realized in the abode of the dead, engulfed in flames (Lk 16:24).

Nothing clears away like fire. It was by a fire that the apostle Peter showed the true colors of his cowardice (Lk 22:55). Gratefully, the fire of Christ's love remained sufficiently enkindled within him so that it consumed him with bitter tears leading to repentance. The fire of the Passion must burn until nothing is left standing but the cross. The conflagration of Calvary establishes once and for all that Christ is the only true Reality.

Jesus has come for division. He has come to divide what divides us, for every kingdom divided against itself is laid waste (Lk 11:17). Even Satan knows that (Lk 11:18). Jesus wants to separate us from the illusion that we can be happy without God. He burns to divide us from those things that create division: Selfishness, jealousy, pride, anger, and the like. The prediction about what will happen to households indicates that we cannot even love our families adequately apart from the grace of God. To join with Jesus as he makes his way to Golgotha, where his own side will be divided, we must ask what divides us from Christ's sacrifice and pitch it into the fire with the unfruitful trees (Lk 3:9).

It is not enough to love God in our heads. We know how little the Lord thinks of the lukewarm (Rv 3:16). We need to be on fire, actively living the graces of the baptism that with have received — to live with integrity, conviction, fervor, and burning zeal. Jesus was even willing to feel divided from the Father on the cross. That anguish only fortified his resolve to live and die for his Father. In Christ's cross, we resolve all our divisions and receive the baptism that promises Gospel peace.

Twenty-First Sunday in Ordinary Time

The Strength of Salvation
Luke 13:22-30

The question of the day is: What is needed to be saved? Jesus answers by way of analogy, presenting heaven as a house where the Father is the Master. The Master keeps his eye on the only way to enter — the narrow gate who is Jesus Christ.

Thus, we must answer for ourselves: What does it mean to be strong enough to enter the narrow gate? In the Gospel, we see many effects of weakness. The doctors of the woman with the hemorrhage are not strong enough to cure her (Lk 8:43). The contestative lawyers and Pharisees are unable to reply to Christ's question about conduct befitting the Sabbath (Lk 14:6) as well as his remark about paying taxes (Lk 20:26). Weakness and ineptitude distinguish the Milquetoast disciple (Lk 14:29-30). As a consequence, to receive true strength we must eschew human limitations, fatalism, and timidity, and unite ourselves to the Body of Christ. Strength flows from seizing Christ with our mind, embracing his Truth, and expunging all deceit, doubt, and dissent. The irresolute, skeptical, diffident disciple can expect never to be strong enough for salvation; that strength accrues to the committed and self-abandoned.

Christ has already taught us about the kind of strength needed for salvation. He has asserted that to be strong enough we must love mightily: To inherit everlasting life we must love the Lord our God with all our strength (Lk 10:27). To be strong enough means guarding what is most valuable in life (Lk 11:21-22). Such strength is the fruit of humble, heartfelt prayer (Lk 21:36). It remains a supernatural gift that Jesus Christ himself receives in Gethsemane in order to help him to Calvary (Lk 22:43). In short, when we are strong with Christ's strength we become like the house that is strong enough to stand up to the rushing torrents of a flood (Lk 6:48). We become the house invited to enter the house of the Father.

Notice well the objection of the master to those who stand outside the door knocking, pleading their case, and protesting their exclusion: "I do not know where you are from." When we refuse to identify with God with integrity and conviction then we forfeit access to the divine. The high priests, Pharisees, and elders learned this lesson the hard way when they smugly declined to acknowledge the divine origin of John the Baptist's baptism (Lk 20:7). The Master knows where we come from when our will is one with his. The Master knows where we come from when we seek him sincerely, accepting our status as "last" with humility, thankfulness, and self-giving. We "come from" God when we persevere in charity in all things. His reciprocating love makes us "first."

To those without such a steadfast commitment, the Master commands: "Depart from me, all evildoers!" This line comes from Psalm six (verse nine) — a psalm of supplication that beseeches the Lord for salvation according to his kindness. Confidence in God's pity and healing remains the fruit of our willingness to live in conformity to him. Otherwise, we can expect to be "cast out" like the temple traders from the house of the Father (Lk 19:45).

To be saved, we must know where we are from and where we are going — we are from the Father and on our way to the Father. And we must witness that communion authentically to others. To be strong enough for salvation, we must pray for the grace to join Jesus with all our heart, soul, mind, and strength as he makes his way to Jerusalem. For the door to heaven is as narrow as the cross.

Twenty-Second Sunday in Ordinary Time

The Distinguished Guest
Luke 14:1, 7-14

How deeply rooted in human nature is the bane of egotism. Christ witnesses its pathetic display at the Pharisee's dinner table where his fellow guests jockey for an exalted place. Their petty antics betray the pitiful condition of inferiority that continues to afflict people ever since the fall. Adam and Eve were the first to attempt to preempt an inappropriate primacy when they reached for the fruit of the forbidden tree. By their action, they sought to usurp equality with God, putting themselves on the same plane. But Jesus Christ himself, who did not deem equality with God something to be grasped at, remains the only antidote to the insecurity that makes an idol out of individualism.

At the heart of the shameless suppertime scurrying is a deficient understanding of human dignity and honor. Grandiosity dupes us into conceiving of eminence as a limited entity that we must claim before another snatches it away. It tyrannizes our life, emptying us of interiority. We have no care about the quality of our soul as long as we remain obsessed with the way we appear to others. We live intimidated, in fear of demotion, dejection, of being associated with the second-rate. We believe our furtive efforts at self-aggrandizement will establish our high place in others' minds and hearts. All that matters is attaining a prestige that puts others in their place. Everything is done for show.

In fact, Luke tells us that the people were observing Jesus carefully. This is not the first time that the Lord has fallen under such captious scrutiny. Earlier, the scribes and Pharisees had watched Christ to see if he would heal on the Sabbath (Lk 6:7). Toward the end of his life, they send spies to attempt to trap Jesus (Lk 20:20). But more than careful watching is needed to recognize the things of God (Lk 17:20). We possess a right regard for God when we regard reality God's way: With a preference for the lowly, the poor, and the needy.

It begins with ourselves. Trying to get above ourselves leaves us in the lowest place of humiliation (Lk 10:15; 16:15). The "embarrassment" of the downgraded guest resembles the shame the Son of Man manifests towards those who deny him (Lk 9:26) and the confusion Christ's opponents experience when he heals (Lk 13:17). Instead, the Christian approaches the banquet of life willingly recognizing his or her own littleness, powerlessness, and nothingness. We happily assume the lowest place because we deserve nothing more. God rejoices to look with favor on his servants in their lowliness (Lk 1:48).

Thus, he exalts those who cherish humility. Christ's Words today serve as literal fulfillment of the Magnificat: "He has thrown down the rulers from their thrones / but lifted up the lowly" (Lk 1:52). Soon this lesson will be dramatically enacted in the temple with the Pharisee and the tax collector (Lk 18:14).

This is the last dinner we read about Jesus attending in the Gospel before the Last Supper. In commanding us to invite the poor, the crippled, the lame, and the blind to a banquet (Lk 14:21), Christ reveals how he regards us as he invites us to the Last Supper. Christ has been sent to bring glad tidings to the poor (Lk 4:18; 7:22); he promises them the reign of God (Lk 6:20). In the same way, Christ calls the crippled, the lame, and the blind into his Eucharistic presence so that he can heal and transform them (Lk 7:22). We are the ones who benefit from their presence at the banquet. Our exaltation consists in humbly discovering Christ's mercy at work in the most miserable and desperate circumstances of life.

Twenty-Third Sunday in Ordinary Time

Turning and Traveling
Luke 14:25-33

It is so easy to miss the theological richness of the Gospel by dismissing key details as mere literary trifle. For example, today Luke tells us deliberately that Jesus "turned and addressed" the crowds travelling with him. He turns to others in the same way to praise the faith-filled centurion (Lk 7:9) and the penitent woman (Lk 7:44). Jesus turns to reprimand his disciples (Lk 9:55) as well as to instruct them privately (Lk 10:23). Christ turns to face the sinful Peter at the moment of his denial (Lk 22:61). And Jesus turns to the weeping women on the way of the cross (Lk 23:28). In short, Jesus turns whenever confronted with weak or failing faith in order to restore and perfect it. As Christ continues on his journey to Jerusalem today, his turning indicates how much our faith needs reinforcing.

What we hear on Christ's lips may shock us: We cannot be his disciples unless we hate all people, including father, mother, and self. By "hate" Jesus means that we must love all things less than we love him. The command is purely logical, for only union with Christ's love makes it possible for us to love in a sanctified — vs. self-serving — way.

Just as hate leads to love, so does death lead to life. We cannot be Christ's disciples unless we carry our own crosses and come after him (Lk 9:23). To carry our cross means to take hold of the very thing that crucifies us. Practically, it means taking responsibility for the particular unfolding of God's Providence in our life, no matter what it may entail: Suffering, sinfulness, dashed hopes, unfulfilled dreams and longings, etc. As the priest prays to Jesus silently during the Mass, "by the will of the Father and the work of the Holy Spirit your death brought life to the world." To carry the cross means not to cross the will of God at work in our life through the Spirit, but to embrace it.

To delineate this, Jesus gives us two images. The builder constructing a tower symbolizes the threat that grandiosity and impetuousness pose to true discipleship. Faulty discipleship invariably results from bloated self-regard. Just as the failure to factor in inflation can wreck the best building plans, so does self-inflation devastate discipleship. The cost of discipleship remains the full gift of self given to complete the blueprint of God's plan for us.

The analogy of the battle-bound king alerts us to the crucial need for prudence, and the disastrous consequences of living according to rash judgment. Christ's recurring call to renounce our possessions frees us from all the myriad ways we seek false comfort and security in things. The attachment to possessions occludes the providential care of God and makes us oblivious to calamity closing in on us fast.

God does not want us to oppose the advancing King but to receive him. For it is Christ the King who advances to Calvary so that we will partake of his triumph. Luke relates that "great crowds were traveling with Jesus." To travel in this way makes us like those who traveled with Jesus when he raised to life the son of the widow of Nain (Lk 7:11). In the same way, we resemble the risen Christ as he travels with the disciples on the road to Emmaus (Lk 24:15). In sum, if we take up our cross, Christ will raise us to new life. If we renounce all to accompany Jesus to his Passion, he will bless us with the love that never ends.

Twenty-Fourth Sunday in Ordinary Time

The Father's House
Luke 15:1-32

One of the greatest sins any human being can commit is to refuse to enter the Father's house out of self-righteousness. The Pharisees and scribes complain today because of the way that Jesus consorts with sinners. We have already seen the scribes and Pharisees doing this at the beginning of Jesus' ministry (Lk 5:30), and we will soon hear similar grumbling from the crowd (Lk 19:7). The scribes and Pharisees fail to understand that, because of Jesus Christ, nothing prevents human nature from being raised up to something greater even after sin. In fact, in God's permissive will, sin can actually draw forth some greater good that might not otherwise come about. Jesus enters the homes of sinners in order to draw them into the house of the Father. The self-righteousness of the complainers keeps them from grasping this.

Today's three parables focus on three distinct "goods" that proceed from the phenomenon of sin. The first concerns how to understand sin itself. The scribes and Pharisees maintain a fatalistic approach to sin. However, Christ's three parables identify sinfulness with the state of being lost. They seem to affirm that much of human sinfulness can be attributed to weakness rather than malice. What sheep willfully gets lost? And we can pardon the arrogance of the prodigal son because he clearly does not know what is good for him. He is lost even before he leaves. In a way, he needs to leave in order to learn it — *felix culpa*.

Moreover, the parables emphasize how much the recovery of what was lost causes joy. God's response to repentance is rejoicing. Heaven and its angels rejoice over the sole repentant sinner precisely because the penitent prefers the justice of heaven to worldly ways. To welcome the justice of heaven means permitting God to purify us with an act of love that makes us worthy of heaven. If we were not first lost in sin, we might never know just how powerless we are to rejoice heaven outside of the embrace of divine mercy.

And finally, sometimes we need to fall in order to come to our senses about right and wrong — about what is true and valuable. Hence, the wonderful absurdity of the woman spending much of what the coin was worth on a reception to celebrate the finding of the coin. Authentic repentance from sin unmasks our self-righteousness by showing us what we have been saved from. As bad as the prodigal son's sin was, his refusal to return to the father in his moment of desperation would have been even worse. Sin convinces him how much the father can be trusted.

Jesus plainly intends an analogy between the older son and those who are complaining about him. In refusing to approach his brother, who was lost and dead, the older son comes across as the antithesis to the good Samaritan — the true neighbor. Notice how much "neighbors" are a part of each of the three celebrations today. The older son distances himself from them all. So does everyone who refuses to enter the Father's house. Yet, the Father is so rich in mercy that he comes out to plead with us — a verb that is the root of the word "Paraclete." To save us from our self-made, self-righteous hells, the Father offers us life in the Spirit through his risen Son.

Only one other person in the Gospel of Luke runs the way the father does today: The apostle Peter, who runs to the tomb of Jesus Christ, confident that the reconciling mercy he will find there is far greater than his great sin.

Twenty-Fifth Sunday in Ordinary Time

Gospel Resourcefulness
Luke 16:1-13

Like the prodigal son story, Luke gives us yet another parable about squandering property. Curiously, the parable intends not to reprove the steward for his irresponsibility, but rather to promote the resourceful way that he deals with his transgression. In effect, Christ shows us a rectified strategy for dealing with sin.

Unlike the older brother of the prodigal son, unwilling as he was to enter his father's house, the soon-too-be-sacked steward wants nothing more than the welcome of clients' homes. Put out with anger, the older brother puts himself out of his own house. He wills bitterness to evict mercy. Yet, his out-of-place ire only displaces him. The refusal to cast out rage makes him an outcast. For such anger is the privation of imagination. However, we see the opposite at work in the ingenious steward who schemes to find any way in off the streets. While consumed with worry about being turned out, his master marvels at how his wiliness turns out. And the master commends him. Why?

The cunning steward possesses those qualities of character necessary of every disciple in order to approach the seemingly desperate circumstances of the cross. The Gospel suggests three. First of all, the master commends the dishonest steward for acting prudently (wisely). The angel revealed to Zechariah that his son John the Baptist would turn back the rebellious to the wisdom of the just (Lk 1:17). In this disobedient steward, the prophecy comes true. In fact, his rebellion plays a providential role in engaging a wisdom that raises him to a higher way of living. In his divine foresight, God uses sin to bring us to such a place. Redemption transforms disobedient stewards into faithful, farsighted ones whom the Master sets over others (Lk 12:42).

How amazingly the prudence of self-preservation kicks in when threatened. The master's clients pay their bills because they think they are getting something for nothing. By forgoing his own commission, the steward gains an exalted status. Only the challenge of self-sacrifice galvanized his prudence. It does so for us as well.

Moreover, the true disciple remains eminently trustworthy always in everything because there is no "very small matter" that does not matter. Every moral situation stands as a graced opportunity to demonstrate virtue. Every act of dishonesty makes a liar out of us. Christian integrity reaches into the least detail and the most minute undertakings of life. Jesus will soon reemphasize this truth in his parable of the servants and the sums of money (Lk 19:17).

And finally, the human heart was made for love, but it cannot serve opposing masters. The steward learned he could serve either his greed or his desire to survive. Crisis makes a realist out of the man. Likewise, our single-hearted conformity to Christ transforms what we love and the way we love. The dilemma of conflicting personal desires at times enlightens our consciousness and helps purify our hearts. When we live by faith, it blesses us with the Gospel realism we need to embrace Jesus Christ as our only Master and his cross as our true home.

Twenty-Sixth Sunday in Ordinary Time

Living Our Lives for Jesus
Luke 16:19-31

The most appalling thing about the rich man in today's Gospel is not that he is decked out in lavish apparel. Neither is it that the rich man gives himself to gluttonous repasts or that he lives in an opulent house. It is not even that he is a messy eater with ill-mannered pets. Rather, the most ignominious aspect of this story is that the starving, sore-ridden pauper lying at the rich man's door is not some anonymous indigent. The rich man actually knows this poor man's name; from the torment of the netherworld, the condemned man cries out to Abraham: "Send Lazarus. . . ." The atrocity of this tale concerns what the rich man knows and how he uses — or fails to use — that knowledge.

How very many times had the rich man coldly breezed by Lazarus languishing at the gate — enough times not only to learn Lazarus's name, but to remember it. A name expresses a person's essence and the meaning of his or her life. By revealing our name to another, we in effect hand ourself over, entrusting ourself to the other. It makes us accessible by inviting greater intimacy. However, for the rich man, the knowledge of Lazarus's name only steeled his resolve to stay far away and removed from the poor man's plight (until the moment when the rich man himself was in trouble!). In his selfish pursuit of hedonistic pleasures, the rich man does not merely spurn a down-and-out homeless individual — he violates the personal dignity of one known to him in a personal way.

The severe culpability of Lazarus appears in a number of Gospel clues. Luke portrays the rich man as the antithesis of the pity-filled Jesus who stops at the gate of the town in Nain in order to reach out in mercy to one in dire need (Lk 7:12ff). On the surface, the rich man's sumptuous dining resembles the banquet ordered by the prodigal son's father (Lk 15:23-24). Whereas the prodigal father's feast celebrates compassion, mercy, tenderness, and reconciliation, that of the self-absorbed rich man remains a smorgasbord of self-indulgence, carnality, oppression, and injustice. The stern Words of Christ's earlier parable may well apply to this callous, deluded rich man, for this very night his life will be required of him (Lk 12.16 21). Ironically, the only other reference in the Gospel to the kind of torment he suffers is the anguish of Mary and Joseph as they search for the boy Jesus lingering behind in the temple (Lk 2:48). In other words, true torment means being separated from the Son of God.

Lazarus, on the other hand, typifies the blessedness of the hungry ones who will be filled (Lk 6:21). It is for the poor like him that the over-abundance of the multiplied loaves has been gathered up to be distributed generously (Lk 9:17). Moreover, Lazarus is comforted in Abraham's bosom in the same way that John the Baptist comforted the people with his exhortations (Lk 3:18). It is a comfort that leads to Christian conformity.

The import of the parable alerts us to the imperative to live our lives to the fullest in virtue, because after death it is too late. The rich man wants Abraham to send Lazarus — a symbol of Christ — to warn his family. But the Word of God himself has already been sent and spoken. Salvation consists in heeding the Word of God. More information helps no one without a freely chosen, faith-filled commitment to moral rectitude.

Similarly, the rich man presumes that an after-death apparition will induce repentance. However, the case of the other Lazarus who came back from the dead (Jn 11:44) argues to the contrary: The crowds wanted to kill him (Jn 12:10). Only belief disposes us to respond to the risen Christ (Acts 13:40-41). Just as Lazarus longed to eat his fill of scraps, Jesus longs to eat his Passover with those who live their lives to the fullest for him.

Twenty-Seventh Sunday in Ordinary Time

To Live by Faith
Luke 17:5-10

Faith is the openness of heart to God's self-communication in the Holy Spirit. Faith joins the human mind to divine knowing. That is why the apostles must be clear about what they want. To enjoy an increase of faith means to see and do things God's way. To increase our faith we must diminish our willfulness. If the apostles ask for their to hearts be opened, they must first be emptied of everything not of God. To increase our faith means to live by faith — to live like Jesus Christ, united and conformed to Jesus Christ in every conceivable way. An increase of faith requires a willingness to lose our life.

The Gospel of Luke presents us with several paragons of faith (Lk 5:20; 7:9; 7:50; 8:48; 17:19; 18:42). Those who desire an increase of faith have a lot to live up to. But the faith that the apostles ask for is not for themselves; it is also for the Church. Christ attests to this the night before he dies when he informs Peter: "I have prayed that your own faith may not fail; and once you have turned back, you must strengthen your brothers" (Lk 22:32). The Acts of the Apostles abounds with reports of how the faith increased because of the increased faith of the apostles (Acts 2:41, 47; 5:14; 11:24). The faith of the apostles is not about self-aggrandizement. It remains ordered to adding to the number of believers and to the depth of belief.

In this respect, the Gospel underscores three dynamics of faith. First, fully actualized faith has little to do with magnitude. It is so easy for us to mistake faith for a commodity whose value depends on amassed quantity. For the key to Gospel faith is potency, not size. To increase in faith we need only have faith in Faith. Disbelief disbands the more we live with conviction.

Moreover, faith transforms our very self. We reveal who we are by what we say. No wonder, then, that the utterance of faith possesses the power to uproot. Faith endows our word with authority and might. Faith infuses speech with divine efficacy. Faith speaking is God acting. When we open our heart to God's self-communication through faith, faith communicates the very heart of God.

And finally, to grow in faith we must uproot erroneous notions of it just as the mulberry tree gets uprooted. Living by faith is not like contracting a business deal with God. At the same time, Gospel faith means much more than the minimalism of obeying rules — of being law-abiding. Too often we give in to the tendency of the presumptuous servant who expects a reward for fulfilling his obligations. We witnessed that in the older brother of the prodigal son when he protested to his father: "Look, all these years I [slaved for] you . . . yet you never gave me even a young goat to feast on with my friends" (Lk 15:29). If we see ourselves as slaves, we can expect to be treated like slaves.

Graciously, faith regenerates us as the Father's sons and daughters. Our faith increases to the degree that we live in uncompromising humility, acknowledging faith as the tremendous gift that it is, and loving it more deeply in that knowledge. That is what faith commands us to do. In response, God calls his faithful to dine at his table (Lk 12:37; 22:27), not because we deserve it, but because God delights to sup with those so like himself.

Twenty-Eighth Sunday in Ordinary Time

Showing Ourselves to the Priest
Luke 17:11-19

Could it be that the leper cured in chapter five managed to get word to his fellow lepers, thereby filling them with the confidence to cry out today: "Jesus, Master! Have pity on us!"? Their cry is more authoritative than it may seem. On four other occasions (Lk 5:5; 8:24, 45; 9:33) we hear Jesus invoked as "Master," each time by the apostle Peter. In other words, there is an apostolic quality about the lepers' request. It signals that their healing will not be for themselves alone but for the Church.

Like the tax collector in the temple (Lk 18:13) and the friends and women at the crucifixion (Lk 23:49), the ten lepers stand at a distance from the Lord as they make their request. They plead for pity, the kind of pity shown by the good Samaritan (Lk 10:37). These details signify the lepers' humility, self-abandonment, and reverence for Christ. They recognize Jesus as the true Neighbor eager to reach out to them in their need. Their healing reveals three key truths about how God acts in our life.

Notice, first of all, that nothing spectacular or glorious happens. Jesus replies to the lepers' plea with the simple instruction: "Go show yourselves to the priests." The lepers could conceivably interpret Christ's words as a rejection. However, their healing will appear as the fruit of their obedience — an obedience that emulates that of Christ. For today Jesus is continuing his journey to Jerusalem, and the lepers are healed as they are going to the priests. Healing often happens on the way. God's intervention in our life is not distinct from the living of our life. Rather, God reveals his saving power while we are en route. The more we implement the words of Christ in confident, devoted compliance, the more do we realize his cleansing power in our life. The lepers' deference attests to Jesus' Messiahship (Lk 7:22). Personal healing relies on the fidelity of our religious acts.

Moreover, the one leper who returns manifests that his healing goes beyond the physical. The encounter with Christ makes him a believer, signified by the acts of returning, glorifying, prostrating, and thanking. The leper's return mirrors that of the exorcised man (Lk 8:39), the jubilant seventy-two (Lk 10:17), the women from the tomb (Lk 24:9), the Emmaus disciples (Lk 24:33), and the Eleven after the Ascension (Lk 24:52). In other words, the leper exhibits the fullness of his faith in missionary fervor.

As the leper falls at the feet of Jesus, his posture recalls the homage of Peter (Lk 5:8), their fellow leper (Lk 5:12), the Gerasene demoniac (Lk 8:28), Jairus (Lk 8:41), and the woman with a hemorrhage (Lk 8:47). Such is the mien of grace rooted in the hope of God's mercy.

The reality of the leper's spiritual healing emerges in the keyword of his reunion with Christ: Thanks. Unlike the thanks of the self-deluded Pharisee praying in the temple (Lk 18:11), the leper's thanks are pure because of the illumined way they transcend the letter of the law. Christ has commanded the lepers to show themselves to the priests. The thanksgiving leper recognizes Jesus as the Only High Priest. He returns to show himself to Christ, the Great High Priest, in the same way that the risen Christ returns to show his wounds to his apostles (Lk 24:40). In this way, the thanks offered by the sanctified leper anticipate the thanks offered by Christ the Priest at the Eucharist (Lk 22:17, 19).

And finally, the authenticity of faith supersedes everything that threatens to preclude the leper from God's favor — he is a Samaritan. Like Peter in Gethsemane, Christ commands us to stand up in that faith and be on our way — which is his way to the cross.

TWENTY-NINTH SUNDAY IN ORDINARY TIME

THE COVENANT OF PRAYER
Luke 18:1-8

Jesus offers special counsel about praying without becoming weary because the quality of Gospel prayer depends on the condition of our heart. The heart of prayer is praying with our heart. If our heart is far from God or if we lose heart because of weariness, then the words of our prayer get uttered in vain.

For Christian prayer is more than an isolated act. It *is* our covenant relationship with God in Jesus Christ. No wonder Luke recounts the many times Jesus prays in the Gospel: After his baptism (Lk 3:21), after curing the leper (Lk 5:16), before calling the apostles (Lk 6:12), before confirming his identity as Messiah (Lk 9:18), at the Transfiguration (Lk 9:28-29), before teaching his disciples the Our Father (Lk 11:1), and before his Passion (Lk 22:41-45). In short, Jesus prays throughout his life at all the key moments of his life. Prayer accompanies and mediates all the ways that Christ manifests the saving love of the Father to his people.

Christ's parable today reveals three key aspects of Gospel prayer. First of all, we are to pray "always." Jesus already signaled the constancy required in prayer in teaching his disciples to pray, "Give us *each day* our daily bread" (Lk 11:3 [emphasis added]). The father of the prodigal son tells his older son: "You are here with me always; everything I have is yours" (Lk 15:31). The always of prayer prevents us from regarding ourselves as slaves by keeping us mindful of our communion with the Father as sons and daughters. The always of prayer gives us access to all the riches of the Father. Everything that belongs to the Father accrues to us because of prayer. Confidence in this truth fills us with the fervor of the Eleven who were "continually in the temple praising God" (Lk 24:53).

Second, the Lord wants us to be clear about how much God revels in incessant prayer. Whereas the bad judge despises the badgering of the widow, the good God delights in the persistence of his chosen ones. The judge capitulates to the widow's request out of exasperation. But it gladdens God to grant our petitions. Our insistent asking insures greater intimacy with God. That is why God himself insists on perseverance in prayer. The judge yearns to be rid of the widow. The Father longs to be one with us. What would exasperate mere mortals gratifies the heavenly Father. Authentic prayer behooves us to abandon inadequate human standards in this regard.

In fact, inconstant prayer invariably diminishes our own fear of God and our respect for others. But the regular practice of prayer transforms us, filling us with the holy fear we find in the good thief (Lk 23:40) — so lacking in the judge. It endows us with the proper respect all people should have for God's Son (Lk 20:13). And that delights the Father.

And finally, prayer stands as an unending epiphany. Jesus laments: "When the Son of Man comes, will he find faith on earth?" He will find it in the faithful at prayer. The Gospel equates failure in faith to the sleep that prevents us from praying (Lk 22:45). Conversely, to pray is remain like those wide-awake servants awaiting their master's return (Lk 12:35-37). Like them, our reward for faithful prayer is to be seated at the Master's table where he waits on us.

Thirtieth Sunday in Ordinary Time

Honest Sinners
Luke 18:9-14

Jesus continues his instruction on prayer today with parable of the Pharisee and the tax collector. Christ places special focus on those who pride themselves on their own righteousness — the nemesis of prayer.

"Righteousness" is a recurring theme in the Gospel of Luke. Two key men at the beginning and at the end of Jesus' life are described as being righteous: Simeon (Lk 2:25) and Joseph of Arimathea (Lk 23:50). Christ declares emphatically that he has not come for the sake of the self-righteous (Lk 5:32). The self-righteous bring no joy to heaven (Lk 15:7). Jesus upbraids the Pharisees for their self-righteousness (Lk 16:15). The enemies of Christ masquerade as righteous men in order to ambush him (Lk 20:20). And when many of those surrounding the Lord have succumbed to self-righteousness, a gentile at the cross confesses Jesus Christ as righteous (Lk 23:47). In short, righteousness leads to the kind of contempt that Jesus himself will experience at the hands of Herod (Lk 23:11). It endeavors to murder God.

As a result, Christ's Words today should come as no surprise. The Pharisee — the poster boy of self-righteousness — totally lacks any sense of sin. While he may not be greedy, dishonest, or adulterous, he *is* prideful, judgmental, unctuous, grandiose, vain, conceited, haughty, arrogant, boastful, and uncharitable. There is plenty wrong that needs contrition and confession.

The paradox lies in the way that the Pharisee prides himself in not being "like the rest of humanity." In this regard, the Pharisee disassociates himself with Jesus himself who, by his baptism (Lk 3:21-22), deliberately identifies himself with sinners. In fact, Jesus has come to save only those who acknowledge their sinfulness (Lk 5:32). The pretentious thanks the tax collector sputters seems to mock the heartfelt thanks of the healed leper (Lk 17:16).

On the other hand, there is the tax collector — one of many who make their appearance in the Gospel (Lk 3:12; 5:27, 29, 30; 6:15; 7:29, 34;

15:1; 19:2, 5, 8). The gravity of the tax collectors' sinfulness is offset by their willingness to listen to the Gospel and to welcome Jesus into their homes. They remain receptive, docile, contrite, disposed. They are honest sinners.

Luke portrays this tax collector in the light of both the lepers (Lk 17:12) and the friends of Jesus at Calvary (Lk 23:49): all of them stand off at a distance — a sign of humility and reverence. He refuses to raise his eyes to heaven to signify his shame and repentance. Christ himself raises his eyes to preach the Beatitudes to his disciples (Lk 6:20). In his sinfulness, the tax collector demonstrates how undeserving he is of such blessedness. Yet, he beats his breast (Lk 23:48) humbly hoping for a mercy he cannot merit.

Because he chooses the lowest place in the temple and humbly offers himself to God in his lowliness, Christ exalts him (Lk 14:11). In the last days, he will be one of those invited to stand erect and hold his head high (Lk 21:28). His justification consists in going home from the temple like Jesus in the company of Mary and Joseph (Lk 2:51) — that is, as another Christ. And just as tax collectors so often invited Jesus to dine at their tables, Jesus invites humble, justified ones who live with a healthy sense of sin to the table of the Last Supper.

THIRTY-FIRST SUNDAY IN ORDINARY TIME

SEEKING AND SOUGHT
Luke 19:1-10

He who exalts himself shall be humbled. Zacchaeus finds this out the hard way after exalting himself up a tree. The Gospel gives us a surprising number of details about this man. Zacchaeus starts with two strikes against him: He is a tax collector and he is wealthy. God destines to send away empty the self-satisfied wealthy (Lk 1:53). Jesus pronounces against the rich who seek their consolation in the present (Lk 6:24). Christ's parables berate the foolishness of the self-content (Lk 12:16-21) and underscore the torment they incur on themselves (Lk 16:19-31). The hope of the wealthy lies in giving what they have to the poor (Lk 18:22) and in living with the self-abandonment of the poor (Lk 21:1). Zacchaeus' willingness to do just that earns him Christ's special attention today.

Zacchaeus was seeking to see Jesus. Christ commends those who seek (Lk 11:9-10). However, such seeking must go beyond mere curiosity. Rather, Jesus stops for us when we seek the Father's kingship over us (Lk 12:31). In his shortness, Zacchaeus ironically resembles the least one who becomes the greatest and who must be welcomed (Lk 9:48). Jesus does just that.

Jesus stops and looks up. When Christ looks up in the Gospel, loaves and fishes become a feast for five thousand (Lk 9:16) and Jesus witnesses the nonpareil of generosity (Lk 21:1). In effect, Christ's glance maximizes Zacchaeus, moving him to a generosity as radical as that of the widow in the temple.

When Zacchaeus hurries down from the tree, his action imitates that of the Blessed Virgin Mary hastening to visit Elizabeth (Lk 1:39) as well as that of shepherds rushing to adore Jesus in the manger (Lk 2:16). Thus, the command of Jesus to come down quickly stands as an invitation to enter into Christ's presence and its transforming power. In the same way, the "today" of the Gospel recalls the "today" of Christmas night (Lk 2:11) and the "today" when Christ fulfills the great promises of Scripture (Lk 4:21).

Zacchaeus receives Jesus (Lk 19:6) with the redemptive joy that fills Zechariah (Lk 1:14), the Blessed Mother (Lk 1:28), and the father at the return of this prodigal son (Lk 15:32). However, it causes the self-righteous in the crowd to grumble like the scribes and Pharisees (Lk 5:30; 15:2). Yet, the testimony to the efficacy of supernatural joy is Zacchaeus' utter lack of self-righteousness. He stands his ground as a justified man, unlike the chief priests and scribes who will stand to calumniate and accuse Christ (Lk 23:10). In pledging to give away his possessions, Zacchaeus fulfills Christ's commands about the use of property (Lk 12:15, 33).

In his desire to lose his life for Christ, Zacchaeus saves it (Lk 9:24-25; 17:33). For Jesus has come to save what was lost, like the sheep, the coin, and the prodigal son (Lk 15:6, 9, 24, 32).

"I must stay at your house." To be welcomed by Christ makes us forever welcoming of Christ (Lk 9:47-48). Who knows — maybe Zacchaeus was that unnamed disciple on the road to Emmaus who pleaded with the unrecognized risen Christ: "Stay with us" (Lk 24:29).

Thirty-Second Sunday in Ordinary Time

Angel, Son, Bride
Luke 20:27-38

Anyone truly attentive to the teachings of Christ in the Gospel recognizes how moot is the Sadducees' question today. Jesus has already asserted explicitly that anyone who comes to him without "hating his wife" cannot be his follower (Lk 14:26). Christ intends this injunction not to penalize us, but rather to provide for us. Because of radical detachment and self-surrender to Jesus Christ, our life on earth now becomes a participation in the heavenly life of the resurrected Christ. In the ultimate communion of heaven, our body and our soul belong to Jesus Christ. Thus the absurdity of asking whose wife the many-times-married woman will be. All those "deemed worthy" belong completely to Christ.

However, the query does offer Jesus the occasion to say something about heaven. The fact that a widow serves as the catalyst for the discussion introduces an intriguing theological dimension. With the appearance of Anna at the beginning of the Gospel (Lk 2:36-40), widowhood is identified with holiness. A widow is the beneficiary of Jesus' preeminent compassion and generosity (Lk 7:11-15). In the teaching of Christ, a widow serves as the paradigm of Christian prayer (Lk 18:3-5). And before his Passion, Christ praises the self-abandonment of a widow as the exemplar of quintessential faith (Lk 21:1-4). In other words, in their narrow-mindedness the Sadducees overlook the most significant aspect of the hypothetical widow's life. She is going to heaven because she is holy, and she reveals to us the pattern of holiness by which we may be "deemed worthy" of heaven.

Perhaps the reason why the Sadducees denied the reality of Resurrection is because they possessed an overly abstract concept of it. Jesus Christ links faith in the Resurrection not to an idea or some cosmic state, but to his very Person. In a certain respect, our personal participation in the Resurrection of Jesus Christ identifies us with angels, sons, and a bride.

In heaven we become like angels. To be in heaven means to leave behind our misinformed, malformed egos and become fully the creatures that God has destined us to be. Only in heaven do the elect find their true identity and their own name. Like the angels, the life of the blessed in heaven consists in the perfect possession of the rich fruits of Christ's redemption. The heavenly elect use those fruits joyfully by laboring to fulfill God's will as it pertains to the People of God on earth. They live fully for God by continuing to live for us.

Moreover, the blessed are "children of God" — literally, "sons of God." Whoever loses his life out of obedient love of the Father, like Jesus, will be made alive (Lk 17:33) even as the Son is given New Life: "Why do you seek the living one among the dead? . . . he has been raised" (Lk 24:5-6). All are alive to God as his children, possessed of the divine merits that come to us as our inheritance through the Paschal Mystery. As God's children, we share in the Resurrection through the Holy Spirit who acts in the sacraments of the Body of Christ.

The righteous will live forever with the risen Christ. The Sadducees' question — "Whose wife will that woman be?"— is preposterous because, in a certain respect, all the elect stand before Christ as his Bride the Church. No one marries or is given in marriage in heaven because Christ the Bridegroom espouses himself to all the blessed. Jesus Christ joins himself with his Bride, the Church, in an everlasting covenant — a covenant in which Christ never stops caring for his Bride as his own Body.

Thirty-Third Sunday in Ordinary Time

The Last Days
Luke 21:5-19

As breathtaking as the temple may be, Jesus makes clear that the Last Days will be even more awesome. In order to be ready for that time, to dodge deception, the Lord counsels us in three ways.

First of all, despite the distressing consequences, Christians are called to live in the name of Jesus. The Lord refers to "my name" three times in this Gospel. Cunning enemies who recognize the power of the Name, but who refuse allegiance to it, will arise in an attempt to defraud others. The name of Jesus graces the Gospel of Luke. The angel informs Mary of her child's name (Lk 1:31; 2:21). Non-apostles successfully cast out demons by the power of Jesus' name (Lk 9:49). In fact, to invoke the name of Jesus stands as a confirmatory sign of belonging to the company of Christ (Lk 9:50). The seventy-two rejoice at the way even Satan falls subject to the name (Lk 10:17). And the risen Christ instructs the Eleven to go forth and preach "in his name" (Lk 24:47). Thus, to invoke the name of Jesus remains the hallmark of Christian discipleship. It fills Christ's followers with the might they need to stand up to the worst that hell has to offer.

Second, Christians can expect to be hated and persecuted precisely because they profess the name of Jesus. However, Jesus has come to save us from the hands of all who hate us (Lk 1:71). This is so much so that Christ calls us blessed specifically because others hate us, ostracize us, insult us, and proscribe our names as evil on account of Jesus (Lk 6:22). Christ invests us with the power to love those who hate us (Lk 6:27). Our "hatred" of anyone or anything less than Christ — like parents, brothers, relatives, and friends who will hand us over (Lk 14:26; 16:13) — empowers us to deal redemptively with those who hate us.

In this way, we pattern our life on that of Christ. Jesus admonishes us that opponents will hand us over (Lk 12:58). If we live reconciled to Christ's love we have nothing to fear. On a number of occasions, Jesus warns his disciples that he himself will be handed over (Lk 9:44; 18:32;

22:21-22, 48; 24:6-7, 20). Our union with Christ in the midst of our own persecutions gives us the assurance that Jesus will bless our fidelity by handing us over to the love of the Father (Lk 9:42).

And finally, Jesus promises to reward the perseverance of his faithful in the face of turmoil with the gift of his own wisdom. Those steadfast ones who live with unflinching endurance will be like the stalwart seed that bears a hundredfold fruit through perseverance (Lk 8:15). It is futile to try to prepare our defense beforehand since to be blessed with God's wisdom requires us to be as little and as dependent as children (Lk 10:21). The Lord asks us to believe that the torturous persecutions of our life are part of his divine Providence and that they redound to his glory (Lk 11:49).

CHRIST THE KING SUNDAY

KING FOR US
Luke 23:35-43

Despite the contemptuous skepticism of the sneering crowd, Jesus Christ truly is the Chosen One. This was revealed at the Transfiguration when the voice from a cloud said: "This is my chosen Son" (Lk 9:35). Thus to be the Chosen One, to be Christ, to be King, all mean the same thing: Christ's sovereignty consists in being first and foremost Son. Jesus manifests the majesty of his kingship in the infallible obedience he renders to his Father. Christ learns obedience from what he suffers, for every occasion of derision, rejection, physical affliction, and now crucifixion offers Jesus the opportunity to prove how radical and resolute is his devoted allegiance to the least desire of his Father's will. In such crucifying obedience, Jesus Christ is perfected — that is, he brings about the divinely ordained goal of his human life: To become the Savior of the world through his death on the cross.

The crowd possesses a warped conception of kingship if they expect Christ the King to come down from the cross himself. Only a spineless, shameless king would exploit the privilege of his authority to indulge a self-seeking end. But Jesus Christ did not live his life for himself but for us, and that conviction perdures in his death. The feast of Christ the King exalts this.

No servant can serve two masters (Lk 16:13), and God the Father is the only Master in Jesus' life. In the Christian dispensation, greatness manifests itself in humble service (Lk 22:25-27). Jesus reveals his royalty precisely by refusing to descend from the cross alive. In fact, the crowd's vicious provocation to Christ to "save himself" is tantamount to Satan's temptation of Jesus in the desert (Lk 4:9-12). In both cases they dare Christ to spurn his Father and renounce his Sonship. Jesus' unwavering resolution, motivated by his love for his Father, makes the cross his throne.

Jesus Christ saves us in refusing to save himself from the torture of death. Zechariah prophesied that the Redeemer would save us from the hands of our enemies (Lk 1:71). To do so, Jesus hands himself over to the torments of those enemies. When Jesus proclaimed that he had come to search out and save what was lost (Lk 19:10), Zacchaeus was up a tree. Now from the tree of the cross, Jesus Christ fulfills his promise by refusing to hurry down.

One would think that after hearing the parable of the sums of money (Lk 19:11-27) people would think twice about crossing an unwelcome king. Obviously, the bad thief has not heard this parable. The good thief, on the other hand, asks to be remembered in Christ's Kingdom. The good thief recognizes Christ as one mindful of divine mercy (Lk 1:54). He donates to Christ the King the sincere gift of himself, which disposes him to receive the Covenant that Jesus offers in his Blood (Lk 22:20; 1:72). In fact, the thief's desire to be remembered reflects the memorializing that Jesus commands of us at the Last Supper: "Do this in memory of me." We unite ourselves to the humble confidence of the good thief when, before receiving Holy Communion, we pray: "Look not on our sins, but on the faith of your Church, and grant us the peace and unity of your Kingdom."

Because of the good thief's utter poverty, the reign of God becomes his (Lk 6:20). The thief seeks out the Father's kingship in Jesus before all else (Lk 12:31). In the thief's humility and contrition, he is like the little child to whom the reign of God belongs (Lk 18:16). Thus, he does not taste death until he experiences the reign of God (Lk 9:27).

St. Gregory of Nyssa once wrote: "The soul shows its royal and exalted character in that it is free and self-governed. Of whom else can this be said, save a king? Thus human nature, created to rule other creatures, was by its likeness to the King of the universe made as it were a living image, partaking both in dignity and in name." Christ evinces his kingship in the free and deliberate surrender of his human soul to the Father on Calvary. The feast of Christ the King calls us to conform ourselves to the kingship of Christ so that we too may live in a free, God-governed way. Then the Only Master whom we serve with all our heart, soul, mind, and strength extends to us a share in his own sovereignty as he calls us to his table where he waits on us (Lk 12:37). How happy are those who eat bread in the Kingdom of God (Lk 14:15). Of his Kingdom there will be no end (Lk 1:33).

PART TWO:
REFLECTIONS ON SOLEMNITIES AND ALSO FEASTS THAT MAY FALL ON SUNDAY

Immaculate Conception

How This Can Be
Luke 1:26-38

There is a marvelous correlation between the mystery of the Immaculate Conception and the story of the healing of the lepers in the Gospel of Luke (Lk 17:11-19). The Gospel account of the Annunciation represents the fulfillment of what began at the Blessed Virgin Mary's conception in the womb of her mother, especially in three ways.

First of all, the angel greets Mary with the words, "Hail, full of grace!" Gabriel identifies Mary as one who is the beneficiary of a divine process. In the dynamic of grace, one blessed with special privileges freely and generously turns to another in need. Mary is the recipient of the supreme heavenly beneficence; God's favor becomes her and she becomes God's favor. Jesus himself is filled with this grace (Lk 2:40, 52). Moreover, this same grace imbues the Eucharist in the form of thanks (Lk 22:17, 19). And although God's goodness extends to the ungrateful (Lk 6:35), thankfulness remains the most godly way to ratify the gift of grace (Lk 7:42-43).

Mary expresses thanks for the divine favor shown her at her Immaculate Conception and at the Annunciation with the words: "May it be done to me according to your word." The lone leper who returns to give thanks demonstrates by his praise-giving actions how he recognizes his healing to be an initiation into the life of grace. The graces of the Immaculate Conception accrue to us through our spirit of thankfulness by which we venerate the Mother of God as Full of Grace.

Second, that angel assures Mary that she has "found favor" with God. There is exquisite theological nuance undergirding this assertion. In a certain respect, the shepherds find favor with God by finding God Incarnate in the manger (Lk 2:12, 16). When Mary finds the child Jesus in the temple, she likewise becomes privy to special divine favor that she cherishes in her heart (Lk 2:51). After the Transfiguration, the disciples find divine favor as they find Jesus alone (Lk 9:36). And as the healed leper shows his reverence to Christ, Jesus says: "Has none but this foreigner returned to give thanks to God?" (Lk 17:18). At one time the lepers were kept at a distance because of the hideousness of their disease. But after their cure, the other nine willfully keep their distance from Jesus. Their apathy toward the favor of being united to Jesus Christ is more heinous than their original affliction.

In the Gospel, the Lord laments: "When the Son of Man comes, will he find faith on the earth?" (Lk 18:8). Jesus has commanded us to seek so as to find (Lk 11:9-10). Jesus will find faith on earth in us if we seek to be united in love with the one in whom God uniquely finds favor when she comes to earth: Mary Immaculate.

And third, the angel declares that "nothing will be impossible for God." Because of the Immaculate Conception, human sinfulness no longer stands in the way of full reconciliation and friendship with God. The impurity of our life keeps us asking, "How can this be?" In fact, we cannot understand the truth about purity in the abstract. The healed leper needed to be in the presence of Jesus to understand the mystery of the gift of his new purity. In purity personified — the Immaculate Conception — we come to revere, to desire, and to love the purity to which we are called. God gives us the purity of Mary in order to enable us to see Goodness only in God. He uses our impurity to make us pure, our imperfection to make us perfect. Mary Immaculate makes the impossible possible.

CHRISTMAS

THE REBIRTH OF CREATION
Luke 2:1-14

The birth of Christ at Christmas transforms all of creation. We see it first in the realm of the angels. At the birth of Jesus, the angels act towards mankind like one who discovers only late in life the existence of a twin sibling. In terms of their absolute perfection, from the moment of creation the angels have ranked ahead of human beings in the hierarchy of being. But with the Incarnation, in a certain respect men and women surpass the angels in their privilege, for God never deigned to become an angel. He became a man. And since Jesus became mortal, his believers will spend immortality living like angels (Lk 20:36).

The angels are nearly giddy with joy as they appear to the shepherds. The whole of the angel's life is devoted to ministering to God, especially in the act of unceasing worship. The appearance to the angels comes across as the angels' attempt to bring the shepherds up to speed. If these mortal shepherds are going to live eternally like angels, they need to know from the first instant of the Incarnation what is most important in life: The praise and adoration of God. The Gloria that the angels sing — and that we sing at Mass — is the first Christian choir practice. When the shepherds make their way to the stable, they will already have a fitting hymn to sing to the newborn Savior.

For, once the shepherds encounter the angels, their lives change. In order to find the Infant in Jerusalem, the shepherds must desert their flocks in the field. Christmas shows us how man comes to himself by moving away from himself. Our openness to the infinity of God is what blesses our life with fullness and makes it complete.

However, it requires a great act of trust and abandonment to believe that God will provide the shepherding care needed for the sheep that the shepherds leave behind. But that is the point: The angels appear to the shepherds because the newborn child is the Good Shepherd come to provide for our every need. One of the first human faces that Jesus will behold from the manger is that of a shepherd. Christ sees what he comes to perfect. As we gaze upon the Incarnate Lord, we behold the perfection that we are to become.

Not only angels and people, but animals as well share in creation's rebirth at Christ's birth. Left alone and without the protection of the shepherds, we might fret about their safety. But even sheep enjoy a privileged priority in the Kingdom of God. In fact, if they were not to get lost, at least for a little while, we would never fully understand the mercy of the Good Shepherd who leaves his flock to search out the single lost one in the wasteland, and to carry it home joyfully on his shoulders (Lk 15:4-7). That triumphant return to the Good Shepherd's true fold begins at Christmas.

Without the tending presence of the shepherds, the sheep may feel alone in those dark fields. But because of Christmas, no one is ever alone again. Jesus Christ is with us in our midst — Emmanuel. Because the Son of God has become one with creation as a man, we can at last become ourselves, secure as the found sheep and as exalted as the angels.

THE PRESENTATION OF THE LORD

PRESENTATION TO THE PRESENCE OF THE FATHER
Luke 2:22-40

The presentation of Jesus in the temple stands as a poignant indication of how similar the beginning and the end of the life of Jesus Christ are. Mary and Joseph take Jesus up to Jerusalem. As an adult, Satan will take Jesus up to a height to show him all the kingdoms of the world. But Mary and Joseph's taking of Jesus constitutes a kind of reunion with the Father. In commending their Son to the arms of the Father, they inaugurate the sacrifice whereby Jesus commends himself to the Spirit of the Father (Lk 23:46). This is one sure, anticipatory step that leads Jesus to the paramount height of Calvary where Jesus reveals the Kingdom of God to all who believe.

Jerusalem is where the parents offer Jesus to the Father, and Jerusalem is where the Son will offer himself to the Father. This revelation is essential to the miracle of the Transfiguration (Lk 9:31). Christ is presented in the temple today as the preparation that empowers the disciples to return to Jerusalem filled with the might and the mercy of the Father (Lk 24:47, 52).

The temple in Jerusalem is the place where Jesus experiences the presence of his Father uniquely. That is why the Lord so vigorously expels the traders from the temple (Lk 19:45). When Jesus returns to Jerusalem as a boy, he confirms the commitment to God that is made today: "Did you not know that I must be in my Father's house?" (Lk 2:49). And so do we, united with Mary's offering of her Son. In presenting Jesus to the Father in the temple, Mary is like the widow in the temple whom Jesus commends: She gives God everything she has to live on (Lk 21:1-4).

The devil will tempt Jesus to throw himself off the parapet of the temple in order to test the efficacy of the Father's love. Yet, Christ will prove his security in his Father's love by laying down the temple of his Body to be sacrificed. The seduction of the devil threatens to sabotage our own trust in the Father's Providence and mercy. Therefore, we celebrate the presentation of the Lord in the temple as our way of recommitting ourselves to all that Jesus teaches us in the temple (Lk 20:1; 21.37-38). In his preaching, Jesus will use the example of one praying in the temple to reveal to us what it means to be justified (Lk 18:10). To be rescued from Satan's faith-dashing parapets, we are called to join the sanctified prayer of the apostles who were "continually in the temple praising God" (Lk 24:53).

Anna "comes forward" at the moment that the Mother of God places her Son in the arms of Simeon. The same verb is used to describe the angel coming to the shepherds on Christmas night (Lk 2:9). And the verb is used to describe the coming forward of the two angels to the women at the empty tomb of Jesus (Lk 24:4). In sum, the presentation of the Lord imbues his believers with the power to come forward into the world proclaiming to all who await redemption the Good News of the Incarnation and the Resurrection. The presentation of the Lord calls us to present the Gospel to others so that they will experience the saving presence of Jesus Christ and find their way back to the Father.

St. Joseph, Husband of Mary

Awake, Amenable, and in Love
Matthew 1:16, 18-21, 24a

The Gospel draws a deliberate correlation between Joseph the husband of Mary and the Joseph of Genesis chapters 37-50. For example, both are the sons of Jacob; both are dreamers; both spend time in Egypt; both act as instruments of salvation; etc.

We are told three specific things about Joseph, the husband of Mary. First of all, he awakens after his dream. In this, Joseph does more than simply return to consciousness. Rather, Joseph awakens to a hope rooted in the truth that has been revealed to him: Jesus will save his people from their sins. After the death of Jacob the patriarch, the guilt-ridden brothers of Joseph fear that he will take revenge on them because of their former treachery toward him (Gn 50:15-18). But Joseph responds: "Even though you meant harm to me, God meant it for good, to achieve his present end, the survival of many people" (Gn 50:20). Joseph, the husband of Mary, awakens with the same self-abandoned, magnanimous trust in the ineffable — if disconcerting — Providence of God. Joseph puts aside his hurts, doubts, and frustrations in order to make way for God's salvation according to God's own way.

Second, Joseph does as the angel of the Lord commands him. In his utter, obedient compliance, Joseph reveals how much he lives by faith. He understands that what has been mystically revealed to him is not meant for himself alone but for the salvation of the world. By confidently acting upon the dream, Joseph assures the advent of the salvation of the world, even as the Old Testament Joseph saved Egypt from a famine (Gn 41:1-46). And just as the Genesis Joseph held command over all the people of Pharaoh, Joseph, the husband of Mary, remains the incomparable patron of the Church.

Finally, Joseph took Mary his wife into his home. The same verb is used to refer to Jesus taking Peter, James, and John up a high mountain to witness the Transfiguration (Mt 17:1). Thus, for Joseph to take Mary as his wife means more than to set up house. Rather, it is an act that leads to

145

the most intimate sharing in divine charity. Only at the Transfiguration do the three apostles gain a glimpse of the vision Joseph witnessed in his sleep even before Jesus was born. To take Mary into our homes is to be taken up into the Paschal Mystery. The transfiguration becomes possible because of the wholehearted way that Joseph loves Mary. With the angel's revelation of the mission of the Incarnation, Joseph's love for Mary does not become moot; rather, it becomes one of the means of effecting the redemptive mission.

In Genesis, it is almost miraculous that Joseph is reconciled with his aged father when Joseph brings Jacob to his house in Egypt. So too, by embracing the miracle that the angel reveals to the Gospel Joseph in his sleep, Joseph — and we — partake of the special communion that Mary shares with God the Father. As we take Mary into our homes with the fervor of St. Joseph, we become reconciled to the Father through the fortitude of one who consented to be a father in God's own inimitable way.

THE ANNUNCIATION

Luke 1:26-38

On the feast of the Annunciation we celebrate how docile, loving obedience to God's Word fills us with the grace to change the way we look at life and to embrace Jesus Christ as the truest Reality. Jesus is as close to us as a Mother's love. The coming of Christ into the world redefines the meaning of every single dimension of creation. Everything that exists receives its ultimate meaning from its reference to God Incarnate. Today is the annunciation of the end of all inadequate, futile, and false approaches to life. The conception of Jesus Christ in the womb of the Blessed Virgin Mary transforms our conception of God, of self, and of the world. Because Mary conceives her Son, we are blessed with the ability to conceive of ourselves the way that God does.

The angel Gabriel's Annunciation reveals that Jesus is Savior, divine Son, Priest Prophet, and King. The very thing that the holy archangel announces today the evil angels will strive to denounce throughout Christ's life. Our response to the Annunciation determines whether we regard the Good News as a blessing or as a curse.

The name of "Jesus" that Mary will give to her Son signifies that he is to be the Savior. This prospect terrifies the demon who possesses the man in the synagogue, causing him to shriek the name of Jesus in terror (Lk 4:33-34). Yet, for those who accede to the Annunciation with the humility and selflessness of the Blessed Virgin Mary, the name of Jesus becomes an instrument of transformation. When we announce it with faith-filled conviction, others are healed (Acts 3:6).

The angel reveals Christ's divinity in identifying him with the Most High. The demons attempt to repulse Jesus using this title as well (Lk 8:28). However, once Christ expels them, the man they once possessed becomes an announcer of the Good News (Lk 8:39). The ability to love our enemies mediated to us through the graces of the Annunciation in turn distinguishes us as "children of the Most High" (Lk 6:35).

The angel clues us in to the kingship of Christ by linking him to the throne of David. Jesus himself claims this authority in dealing with the pettiness of his opponents (Lk 6:3; 20:41). The crowd hails Christ as the king-successor in his triumphant entry into Jerusalem (Lk 19:38; Mk 11:10). The bad thief continues from the cross to sputter diabolical denunciations (Lk 23:39), but because of the rectified receptivity of the good thief, Jesus announces the promise of paradise to him (Lk 23:43).

Jesus Christ is the culmination of all the prophets and patriarchs. They enjoy a privileged place in the Kingdom of God where Christ reigns (Lk 13:28). The mystical bond of love transacted between the Holy Spirit and Mary at the Annunciation prophesies the communion that the blessed will share with the God of Jacob, the God of the living in heaven (Lk 20:37).

Perhaps most important of all, at the Annunciation God is revealed as Father. The demons will conspire to undermine Christ's confidence in his Sonship (Lk 4:3-9; 4:41; 8:28; 22:70). But to no avail. For, beginning in the womb of Mary, the Father gives everything over to his Son who wishes to reveal the Father to us (Lk 10:22), even at this moment through the maternal mediation of the Mother of God. The Father will renew this annunciation throughout Christ's life (Lk 3:22).

What the angel Gabriel today intimates to Mary invites us to intimacy with her divine Son. Because of the Blessed Virgin's Mary's consent at the Annunciation, what the Father will declare at the Transfiguration is true of us in a real way today: "This is my chosen Son" (Lk 9:35).

The Ascension

Blessed, Set Apart, Exalted

Luke 24:46-53

St. Augustine makes the point that the humanity of Jesus Christ needed to be taken away from the disciples in order to dispose them to welcome the Holy Spirit. Our human nature can polarize our devotion to the Second and the Third Persons of the Holy Trinity. As long as Jesus remains physically, visibly with us in the manner to which we have become accustomed, our interest and our attention remain exclusively with him. Unless the bodily form of Jesus is taken away from us before our very eyes, we resist taking account of the divine activity of the Holy Spirit. We need a new way of perceiving and appreciating the full offering of the Blessed Trinity. Jesus gives us that in his Ascension.

St. Augustine insists that we cannot become spiritual people unless we cease to be unspiritual. And we cease to be unspiritual today when the Body of Jesus Christ ascends into heaven, whereby the form of God leaves our sight and becomes grafted upon our hearts instead.

There are three components to this great good-bye. First of all, Jesus raises his hands and blesses his disciples. Jesus Christ ascends to heaven as the great High Priest returning to the heights of heaven. This final sacred gesture recalls the blessing that Jesus invokes over the loaves and fishes (Lk 9:16) and over the elements of the Eucharist (Lk 22:17-20). The ascending Jesus blesses his disciples so that they may become instruments of blessing to others. After this event, the Eleven were found in the temple constantly, blessing God (Lk 24:53). Thus, every time the priest raises his hands at liturgy and in prayer, he renews the benediction bestowed by the risen Savior as his farewell gift to us. In this blessing we become truly blessed. And that blessing sustains us when we can no longer see the mortal face of Jesus.

Second, as Jesus blessed his disciples he parted from them. The disciples most likely had not yet fully recovered from the grueling separation from Jesus that they had experienced in those three days after his crucifixion. The prospect of permanently losing sight of the one with whom they had only recently been miraculously reconciled might have seemed too much to bear. That is why Jesus does not disappear in the dark of night, or vanish from the earth while away from the crowds, all alone in the way that he used to pray.

We need to see Jesus withdraw from us. For his parting becomes the exemplar for all the detachment, mortification, and self-denial so crucial to the life of faith. In leaving us, we are not left alone. By his ascending, Christ creates in us a new space that will be filled with the ineffable love of the Father and the Son — the Holy Spirit. Clinging in a worldly way to the Body of Jesus precludes us from living in this superior, otherworldly love. However, by embracing the Ascension we gain the power to let go of everything that is beneath us and the dignity that God desires to shower upon us.

And finally, Jesus is taken up to heaven. In the rising of Jesus we glimpse something of our own exaltation. The Ascension convinces us how important it is to keep our hearts fixed on the things that are above. The more we live looking up to our risen and ascended Savior, the more others will look up to us because of the transcendent witness of our faith. Others will be taken by the way our lives are taken up in the love of Christ.

THE BIRTH OF JOHN THE BAPTIST

REACHING OUT FOR WHAT LIES AHEAD
Luke 1:57-66, 80

The birth of John the Baptist is a miracle. At a time when Zechariah and Elizabeth should have been busy getting their affairs in order and preparing for death, they find themselves instead surrounded with diapers and all the joys attendant upon having a baby in the house. St. Basil wrote that the person who reaches out for what lies ahead of him is always becoming younger than himself. Today Zechariah and Elizabeth are as old as their newborn infant. And so are we as we reach out for what the Lord offers us in the birth of St. John the Baptist.

Today is born the Voice of the Word. To celebrate the nativity of John the Baptist is to re-sensitize our soul to the graces of the Incarnation. The holy day of John's birth reminds us how potent the Baptist's presence is in disposing us to welcome the Lamb of God. And we need that disposition since we are so inclined to become absorbed and sated with very much that has little to do with God. Not many things can stop us in our tracks and get us to reflect and refocus. But the birth of a baby thrills and fascinates. The innocence of an infant reminds us of what we once were; it kindles in us a hope of what we might become, provided that we resist losing sight of what truly matters.

This little boy transforms everyone around him. One can only imagine the anguish suffered by Elizabeth after so many agonizing years of barrenness. Did the neighbors and relatives that assembled for the circumcision today regard Elizabeth as a pariah — as one cursed by God? It is only too likely that her opinion, her insight, was simply dismissed at family gatherings. How could one forgotten by God have anything constructive to say? But the one whose voice may often have been disregarded today gives birth to the Voice that will silence the world's clamoring in preparation for the Word. Elizabeth is the mother of the baptism that the crowd will receive. It is this confidence that fills her with the boldness to insist on God's revelation — her son's name: "He will be called John."

151

This is a kind of birthday for Zechariah. Although the infant Baptist cannot yet speak, his presence in the household restores the voice of his father. The angel Gabriel foretells that John will turn the hearts of fathers to their children (Lk 1:17). At the announcement of John's conception, Zechariah's heart had been filled with distrust. The nativity of John the Baptist summons us to reexamine the quality of our own hearts. In what or whom do we put our trust? How do we define the possible and the impossible? Do we live reaching out for what lies ahead, or do we live turned in and tormented by the failures and defeats of the past? This supernatural birth turns the heart of the father Zechariah to his child so that he — and we — will become the children who inherit the Kingdom of God (Lk 18:15-17). That is why there is no anger or rancor in the newly opened mouth of Zechariah — only the praises of God.

And finally, the wonder of this heaven-sent child fills all the neighbors with fear. Things are not as cut-and-dried as they seem. Facile, convenient ways of explaining the world cannot share the same room with John the Baptist. This fear is good if it fills us with humility and wonder. For then we remain predisposed to receive the answer to our question: "What, then, will this child be?" He will be the one who shows us how to reach out to our eternal destiny: Communion with Jesus Christ.

Saints Peter and Paul

Apostolic Integrity
Matthew 16:13-19

The holy apostles are blessed because of the way they respond to divine revelation. Simon confesses Jesus to be the Christ, the Son of the living God in response to a revelation from the heavenly Father. Saul falls to the ground on the road to Damascus where the Son of God reveals himself to him, saying: "I am Jesus" (Acts 9:5). Simon becomes Peter and Saul becomes Paul, and the Church becomes strong.

This is an age when people readily discount the divinity of Christ and the teachings of the Church, demeaning Jesus to the inadequate status of brother, friend, or role model. However, the holy apostles Peter and Paul proclaimed to their deaths that Jesus Christ is Lord. They knew too well the high price of relativism and compromise. How much Peter suffered as a result of his denial of Jesus by the fire at the beginning of Christ's Passion. Even more, Saul's original rejection of Jesus Christ took the form of persecution and outright murder. Thus, we celebrate the holy apostles in order to repent of all the ways that we deny and disgrace Jesus Christ by our self-absorbed mediocrity.

The weakness and failure of these apostles lay the foundation for their future greatness. The memory of their personal evil prevents them from ever underestimating the horror and deadliness of sin. Peter and Paul realize that to proclaim Jesus Christ authentically is to proclaim his teaching in all its fullness, without alteration, revision, or diminishment. To be united to Jesus Christ is to embrace the teaching of the Church wholeheartedly. That is why Jesus entrusts Peter with the keys to that union.

We continue to rely on those who can witness to the struggle and the triumph of remaining true to Jesus Christ to show us how to live in the truth with unmitigated integrity. Then, thanks to our own apostolic zeal, the one, holy, catholic, and apostolic Church will become just a little bit stronger. We will become a revelation of God to others that moves them to respond in faith.

SAINT PETER AT NEMESIS BEACH

Just as one day
 a sea-striding Jesus
  beckoned a Rock to believe he could be buoyant
   — grace perfecting nature . . . upholding . . . uplifting —
   did Peter return to the faith-lapsing lake?

Perhaps he did, with new spirit and vigor
And — as if to a lame man begging for alms —
 commanded himself before witnessing waters:
  "Without silver or gold, I give what I have:
   In the Name of Jesus Christ, *walk!*"

Then . . . stepped surely
 from the beautiful gate of that steady beach,
  and — like a gleeful Red Sea Hebrew — the apostle
  went skipping across
   a Galilee Sea.

THE TRANSFIGURATION

THE REVELATION OF OURSELVES
Luke 9:28b-36

Jesus Christ reveals us to ourselves and brings to light the exalted dignity of the human person. This happens literally in the glorious light that beams from the transfigured Body of Jesus, revealing his divine Person and our divine destiny.

However, the Transfiguration is as much about speaking as it is about seeing. Moses and Elijah appear in glory in order to converse with Jesus. More specifically, they speak of Jesus' exodus — his redemptive death on Calvary. Witnessing the vision, Peter attempts to add his voice, but he does not know what he is saying. Finally, the Father himself speaks in a voice from a cloud, identifying Christ as his Son and commanding those present to listen to him. Thus, the Transfiguration is an invitation to an unending conversation with Jesus Christ the Word. To appropriate the mystery of the Transfiguration means to cultivate a spirit of recollection that keeps us listening and contemplative.

No wonder Peter, James, and John "fell silent" at the resounding of the Father's voice. In such silence Zechariah is formed and perfected to become the father of the forerunner of Christ (Lk 1:20). Prayerful silence before the Mystery transforms the world. It readies us to speak courageously about the cross, about sinfulness, and about the need for salvation in the blood of Christ. Without such recollection, like Peter we do not know what we are saying. However, when we remain deeply united to Christ, we need not worry about what to say because the Holy Spirit himself teaches us what should be said (Lk 12:11-12).

And speak we must. Authentic contemplation leads to action, our silence to faith-speaking. As the discourse of Moses, Elijah, and the Father himself makes clear, God relies on the efficacy of language and communication to draw others into the Paschal Mystery. Pope John Paul II has remarked that the phenomenon of the Word is a fundamental dimension of our spiritual experience which brings us back to the ineffable mystery of God himself. To consider the Transfiguration without reference to what is said is like watching television with the sound off — we see, we are intrigued, but we cannot really understand or enter in.

Jesus assures us that each person speaks from his heart's abundance (Lk 6:45). What we say reveals how much we are united to the mystery of the Transfiguration — how much that mystery transfigures us. Transfiguration fuels evangelization. The more we speak about Jesus Christ and him crucified, the more do we experience the supernatural presence of Christ, as did the Eleven: "While they were still speaking about this, he stood in their midst" (Lk 24:36).

Our devout witnessing, listening, and speaking in turn transfigure us. At the Transfiguration, a shadow covers the apostles. But after the Resurrection, the people yearn to have the shadow of the transfigured Peter fall on them (Acts 5:15). Peter and John astound the Sanhedrin with their other-worldly self-assurance: "Whether it is right in the sight of God for us to obey you rather than God, you be the judges. It is impossible for us not to speak about what we have seen and heard" (Acts 4:19-20). With Peter and John, the young Church reveres James as one of its acknowledged pillars (Gal 2:9). Such is the effect of uniting ourselves to Christ's Transfiguration.

The Assumption

Mary's Total Gift of Self
Luke 1:39-56

There are remarkable similarities between the mystery of the Visitation and that of the Assumption. In both cases, the Blessed Virgin Mary is on the move. To bring about the Visitation, Mary sets out and travels to the hill country of Judah. On the day of the Assumption, the body of the Mother of God sets out from her tomb and is lifted up to the high place of heaven. The motion that characterizes the mystery of the Assumption symbolizes our dynamic, transporting relationship with God. Just as Mary is elevated to a sharing in the communion of the Blessed Trinity, so does she pray that God will lift up the lowly.

It is so easy to think of belief as something inert, static, staid. On the contrary, to live by faith is to live in a vital, energetic, pro-active way. Those who resolutely commit themselves to Jesus Christ, the Way, are going places. As the Mother of God heads toward heaven today, her entrance helps to heal all that is untoward in us. Mary's approach to heaven draws us closer to our salvation. St. Louis de Montfort wrote that to be entirely and truly devout toward Mary and devoted to her is an infallible sign of predestination. In this movement of Assumption, Mary models how the Church, the Body of Christ, exists in a continuous process of resurrection to new life. As Mother, Mary calls us to be part of it.

Elizabeth is stunned by the visitation of her guest: "How does this happen to me, that the mother of my Lord should come to me?" The Assumption of the Blessed Virgin Mary lifts us above our feelings of inferiority and worthlessness. In our increasingly impersonal, even inhumane world, we become saturated with a sense of insignificance. When we lose contact with Jesus Christ, we forfeit the meaning of our very selves. In this pathetic state we adopt a kind of "herd mentality" — living as a crowd of individuals, each of whom lacks a real "self." In such a state we have no self to give others, and Christ's summons to live selflessly seems superfluous at best.

That is why Mary's entire self is assumed into heaven: To restore our personal contact with Jesus Christ in the way that we originally experienced it — via the body and soul of the Mother of God. In Mary's Assumption we discover our uniqueness in God's eyes. In Mary's Assumption we rejoice in the dignity that the world tries to assassinate. In Mary's Assumption we delight in making a total gift of ourselves. Just as Mary's whole self is assumed into heaven, so is every moment on earth an invitation to be wholly self-giving. To do so is a joy and not a hardship, for we continue perpetually to hear the greeting of Mary as did Elizabeth, filling our bodies and souls with the transforming grace of her Son.

Finally, Elizabeth exclaims: "Blessed is the fruit of your womb." In heaven, the womb of the Mother of God continues to be fruitful. Blessed Guerric of Igny wrote: "Mary is a mother of all who are reborn to life. Her womb carried a child only once, yet it remains ever fruitful, never ceasing to bring forth the fruits of her motherly compassion." Mary sings from the depth of her Immaculate Heart: "[God] has remembered his promise of mercy . . . to Abraham and his children forever." God continues to realize his promise of mercy through the maternal mediation of the Blessed Virgin Mary assumed into heaven. Whenever the world gets us down we need only look up to heaven to receive the uplifting love of our Mother whose presence with the saints and angels fills our aching soul with the hope of future promise.

Triumph of the Cross

The Triumph of the Cross in Us
John 3:13-17

If for no other reason, we need Jesus to be lifted up on the cross so that we can look up to him in his death throughout our lives to know how to live. If we believe that by dying on the cross Jesus Christ saved the world from the ravages of sin, then why do we continue to sanction sin's insidiousness? Every act of hate, of violence, of impurity, of deceit, of selfishness, of greed, of malice, of apathy, of vindictiveness, of self-indulgence, of heartlessness makes a mockery out of the cross of Jesus Christ. Such action betrays that we have allied ourselves with another ideology, another ethic — a mythology — at odds with the cross of Jesus Christ.

Any time that Christians give way to jealousy, entitlement, anger, prejudice, vanity, viciousness, vengeance, dishonesty, complaining, cowardice, laziness, self-righteousness, laxism, sentimentality, or pride they create a contradiction that derides the very cross of Jesus Christ. To live without praying is to repudiate the cross of Jesus Christ. Whenever we take our eyes off that cross, what is worst about our human nature kicks in. God becomes optional, decorative, quaint, obsolete, inept.

We cannot exalt the cross of Jesus Christ unless we allow it to triumph in our every motive, desire, impulse, understanding, thought, and intention. The exaltation of the holy cross remains the very definition of Christian discipleship. To exalt the cross of Jesus Christ is to embody the very truth that Jesus Christ died for. To exalt the cross of Jesus Christ means denouncing the culture of death, rejecting the legion false gods of the world, repulsing every urge to cower or compromise because of our Christian convictions, and living with radiant, irreproachable integrity.

Every single action of our life should proclaim to the world that we belong to Jesus Christ and that we live only for him. But so many of us are so easily duped and seduced by the guile and the wiles of the world. We give in to infamy without even realizing a battle has been waged.

We need the cross of Jesus Christ in our lives, on our bodies, before our eyes, physically signed in our prayer at every moment of every day.

Without it we are lost. In essence, the cross symbolizes the way that we respond to temptation in our life. When confronted with our weakness, vulnerability, and limitation, we prefer to cross the cross out of our life and to live according to our own ideas, our own resources, our own predilections, our own will and whim. We think that by ignoring it we can avoid the cross althogether. And perhaps we can if we content ourselves crassly with the world and the worldly. But if we long to go up to heaven, we must unite ourselves to the one who has come down from heaven and who returned there again by way of the ladder of the cross.

Accordingly, God insists on permitting the "temptation" of the cross as his providential way of keeping us aware of his divine presence in our lives — especially at the darkest moments — so that we will abandon trust in our own paltry strength and confide ourselves fully to the Father. To attempt to avoid the cross is to spurn Jesus Christ and the Father's love. "God so loved the world that he gave his only Son." Before receiving Holy Communion at Mass, the priest prays inaudibly: "Lord Jesus Christ, Son of the living God, by the will of the Father and the work of the Holy Spirit your death brought life to the world." Only in the cross of Jesus Christ does the true meaning of "reality" come to light. Every secular, self-centered thing outside of the cross only continues Christ's crucifying.

The cross of Jesus Christ is exalted when we give ourselves back to the Father in the same love with which he gave us his Son. We exalt the cross of Jesus Christ whenever we glorify the Father by relying on him, and him alone, in our weakness.

ALL SAINTS' DAY

THE HOLINESS OF THE BLESSED TRINITY
Matthew 5:1-12a

According to the Beatitudes, the conditions for sainthood involve both negative and the positive elements. Why does Jesus call the poor in spirit, the mourning, the meek, the hungry and thirsty, and the insulted and persecuted blessed? It is because these are the ones who, in their neediness, remain open and disposed to the intervention of God. Self-sufficiency remains the nemesis of sanctity. The hallmark of holiness is humility, that is, an unfailing acknowledgment of our nothingness that keeps us constantly and confidently dependent on divine graciousness as God's sons and daughters.

Simple logic discloses the supreme wisdom in this. Being subject to no one remains the preeminent privilege of the prosperous. The self-serving rich revel in relying on no one else. In this way, those caught up in wealth become a kingdom unto themselves (Mt 19:23-24). Thus, to the affluent, Christ's offer of the Kingdom of heaven is immaterial.

To mourn bespeaks a tender heart devoted to another. At the same time, the heart of the disciple must remain wholly fixed on Jesus Christ. This requires a radical detachment from those we would otherwise love most in the world (Mt 19:29-30). Thus, mourning is an essential step in the process of perfecting the heart for holiness. When we unite ourselves to Jesus with the same love that with which a bride receives her groom, the comfort of Christ's constant presence displaces our mourning (Mt 9:15).

Meekness bespeaks holiness because it embraces an authentic self-knowledge and love of littleness. Grandiosity, the opposite of meekness, foolishly vies for the power and prestige that uniquely befit God. By their haughtiness, the grandiose make an island out of themselves. But the meek inherit the land in order to populate it with the greatness of God, and not with monuments to self.

Hunger and thirst are unavoidable in life. But when we refuse the craving to cater to the carnal and the venal, and we respond rather by pursuing righteousness, the holiness of Christ becomes our satisfaction. Conversely, the experience of insult and persecution, which seems so pointless and debilitating, gains us a place in the Kingdom that we could not attain without suffering.

At the same time, Christ exalts three positive qualities of the saints because they reflect three concrete attributes of the holiness of the Blessed Trinity. The merciful are called blessed because of the way that they image God the Father, who is rich in mercy (Eph 2:4; 1 Pt 1:3). The omnipotence of God is manifested in his mercy. Since the Father loves us by being merciful, he rewards the compassionate with the mercy that is most like himself.

The pure of heart enjoy blessedness because they image the obedience of the Sacred Heart of the Son, who identifies himself as "meek and humble of heart" (Mt 11:29). Since the single-hearted settle for nothing less than the goodness and love of God, they are rewarded with the vision of God. When the saints possess the purity of heart of the Son, the Son responds by showing them the Father (Jn 14:9).

And Christ proclaims blessed the peacemakers because of their likeness to the Holy Spirit. The saints embody the Spirit's tendency toward life and peace (Rm 8:6). On Pentecost day, the risen Jesus blesses his disciples with peace as he breathes on them the Holy Spirit (Jn 20:21-22). The blessedness of the saints consists in mediating that reconciling peace whereby others are begotten of the Spirit (Jn 3:5). The saints' reward is to remain ever like the children of God they help others to become.

ALL SOULS' DAY

THE SOUL OF LOVE
Matthew 11:25-30

All things have been handed over to the Son of God by the Father, including the souls of those who have died in need of further purification in order to enjoy the Beatific Vision of heaven. No one knows the Father except the Son. Thus, the Son offers the threefold invitation of the Gospel to the holy souls of Purgatory so that they will know the Father in ultimate communion.

Jesus beckons, "Come to me." Life is about making fitting choices that lead us to God. Purgatory strips away those remaining layers of egoism and individualism that keep us isolated and closed in on ourselves. In calling us to heaven, Jesus calls us out of our selves and out of our self-centeredness. We labor under so many grandiose delusions about our own superiority and greatness. The purification of the holy souls is a kind of humility in which, once and for all, we claim and love Jesus Christ as the center and meaning of life. We can go to heaven only after coming to Jesus in the very way that the Son approaches the Father — in utter self-giving.

Jesus summons, "Take my yoke upon you." The objective of our life is not to accumulate virtues like so many trophies. We persist in the fallacy that we can "take it with us" — our worldly possessions and accomplishments. However, the fulfillment of life lies in preparing for the ultimate act of dying. Each moment of life is meant to be a kind of death whereby we die to all that is not of God in God's love and for his love. St. Ignatius of Antioch once wrote: "Unless we are ready through Christ's power to die in the likeness of his Passion, his life is not in us." In the purification of purgatory, the holy souls place their focus fully and completely on the cross of Jesus Christ — the key to finding eternal rest. To take Christ's cross upon ourselves is to displace all the other lesser things that clamor for our attention.

And Jesus commands, "Learn from me." What do the holy souls learn in purgatory? In purgatory we learn the full truth about ourselves without recourse to rationalizations or excuse-making. In purgatory we learn the full truth about Jesus and the love of God. There, perhaps for the first time, we experience our impurity within the purity of God. On earth it is so easy to dismiss presumptuously the evil of our impurity as harmless and inconsequential. Yet, we cannot enter into the bliss of heaven until we grasp how God wishes to be loved — in the truth who is himself. For that is what makes heaven heavenly. Purgatory terminates when we become emboldened to see ourselves as God sees us, and when God's love becomes who we are. Then our isolation ends and the soul can enjoy the company of loved ones in the definitive community of heaven. For then we have learned to love even as we are loved.

DEDICATION OF ST. JOHN LATERAN BASILICA

THE TEMPLE AND THE TEMPORAL
John 2:13-22

From the moment of his conception, Jesus' most profound earthly experience of his Father is in the person of his Mother and in his own human body. Christ's entrance into the temple — at his presentation, when he lingers behind as a boy, and today when he cleanses the temple (the first time that Jesus goes to the temple in the Gospel of John) — is for the Son of God an overwhelming encounter with the presence of his Father. For Jesus, to set foot in the temple is to enter into the Father's embrace in a temporal way. Jesus explicitly identifies the temple with his Body because his Body remains the concrete way that the Father manifests his redemptive love to the world. At the same time, precisely through his bodiliness, everything about Christ's whole earthly life is Revelation of the Father.

While Jesus' words today about destroying and then raising up the temple may mystify Christ's enemies, they speak clearly and distinctly to us who love him. We know that Jesus means much more than the miraculous reconstruction of a mere edifice. Because Christ identifies the temple, and all it signifies to him about the Father, with his own Body, Christians henceforth build churches — temples — to further that identification in their own lives of faith. Church buildings are more than "places"; rather, they are sacred means of entering into the union that Jesus shares with his Father, and that he makes available to us in the Incarnation. That is what we celebrate today as we commemorate St. John Lateran Basilica, the cathedral church of Rome.

In the Body of Jesus Christ, we see three ways that the Father makes present his merciful love for his people. First of all, in the physical body of Jesus Christ the love of the Father becomes for ever visible. "God so loved the world that he gave his only Son, so that everyone who believes in him might not perish but might have eternal life" (Jn 3:16). The Father gives his Son to us bodily so that in his incarnate flesh we might find the way to the Father.

Christ violently cleanses the temple because the vendors there prefer the carnal to the Incarnate. They sacrilegiously co-opt the good things of creation in order to further their own pernicious ambition. For them, the temple is not a place to encounter the Father but rather a gross way to increase their gross. The treacherous action of the merchants in the temple anticipates the way that the crowds will violate the temple of Christ's Body in the Passion.

Second, the Body of Christ is the means by which the Father sanctifies us in the Spirit. The first disciples approach Jesus and ask, "Where are you staying?" (Jn 1:38). Jesus shows them, not a place, but himself. He invites them to sanctifying communion with himself. Holy communion with Christ's Body remains essential to staying with Jesus and to sharing in the union of love he lives with his Father. "Unless you eat the flesh of the Son of Man and drink his blood, you do not have life within you" (Jn 6:53). The open side of Christ on the cross silently reaffirms the command that Jesus issues the night before he dies: "Remain in me, as I remain in you" (Jn 15:4). Living in the Church, the Body of Christ, is the source of our holiness. It is where Jesus stays.

And third, the Father saves us by raising up the Body of Christ. In a certain respect, the empty tomb (Jn 20:12) stands as a prototype of the Lateran Basilica and every Catholic Church. The appropriate reverence we show it recalls and participates in the extraordinary veneration that Joseph of Arimathea demonstrated in asking Pilate for the body of Jesus (Jn 19:38-42). Joseph claims Christ's dead body in an act of hope. By binding himself to the Body of Jesus he binds himself to the Church — the meaning of "religion."

CONCLUSION
DOCTRINAL PREACHING

The philosopher Soren Kierkegaard once wrote that everyone who in truth wants to serve the truth is *eo ipso* in some way a martyr. But who of us wants to die? Yet, the Words of Jesus Christ continue to resound: "Whoever is ashamed of me and of my words in this faithless and sinful generation, the Son of Man will be ashamed of when he comes in his Father's glory with the holy angels" (Mk 8:38).

WHY THE CHURCH NEEDS DOCTRINAL PREACHING

Nonetheless, too often preachers abandon doctrinal preaching for predication pronouncedly psychological, sentimental, pietistic, polemical, or moralizing. This preference can have disastrous consequences. The great preacher, St. John Chrysostom, recognized this and inveighed against it in an instruction on preaching:

> Let a man's diction be beggarly and his verbal composition simple and artless, but do not let him be inexpert in the knowledge and careful statement of doctrine. Anyone who has the responsibility of teaching others must be experienced in doctrinal conflicts. He himself stands secure and is not injured by his opponents. Yet, when the multitude of simpler folk who are set under him see their leader worsted and unable to answer his opponents, they do not blame his incapacity for the defeat, but his unsound doctrine. So through the inexperience of one man the whole congregation is brought to ultimate disaster. Though they may not quite join the enemy, they cannot help doubting where they used to be confident. Those whom they used to consult with unwavering faith they can no longer attend to with the same security.

Thus, according to Chrysostom, masterful knowledge of doctrine precedes the exigencies of eloquence. In fact, the preacher's doctrinal erudition effectively compensates for any rhetorical defectiveness.

This compromised attitude opens the door to fideism — a position that dismisses the propositions of faith as inadequate, dispensable symbols of an "actual" faith acquired independently of conceptual dogmas. Fideism contests the intellect's capacity to secure certain knowledge of divine matters, especially via doctrine. Instead, it relies on the conviction of the heart to attain salvation.

At the opening of the Second Vatican Council, Pope John XXIII foresaw this threat to the faith:

> Catholic doctrine must be known more widely and deeply, and souls must be instructed and formed in it more completely; and this certain and unchangeable doctrine, always to be faithfully respected, must be understood more profoundly and presented in a way which meets the needs of our time (quoted in *Fides et Ratio*, 92).

Cardinal Christoph Schönborn has stressed in *Introduction to the Catechism of the Catholic Church*: "We are badly in need of an up-to-date account of doctrine's place in a complete education in faith. This would require overcoming a still very strong emotional antipathy to doctrinal catechesis" (San Francisco: Ignatius Press, 1994, p. 55).

THE SCOURGE OF MORALISM

In his encyclical *Fides et Ratio*, Pope John Paul II warns against a simplistic pragmatism regarding doctrine that results in reductionism. He writes: "The temptation always remains of understanding the revealed truths of faith in purely functional terms. This leads only to an approach which is inadequate, reductive, and superficial at the level of speculation" (97). This reductionism often appears in the form of moralism.

Cardinal Joseph Ratzinger addressed this tendency in a recent speech:

> The temptation to turn Christianity into a kind of moralism and to concentrate everything on man's moral action

has always been great. For, man sees himself above all. God remains invisible, untouchable and, therefore, man takes his support mainly from his own action. But if God does not act, if God is not a true agent in history who also enters into my personal life, then what does redemption mean? Of what value is our relationship with Christ and, thus, with the Trinitarian God? I think the temptation to reduce Christianity to the level of a type of moralism is very great indeed even in our own day. . . . For we are all living in an atmosphere of deism. Our notion of natural laws does not facilitate us in believing in any action of God in our world. It seems that there is no room for God himself to act in human history and in my life. And so we have the idea of God who can no longer enter into this cosmos, made and closed against him. What is left? Our action. And we are the ones who must transform the world. We are the ones who must generate redemption. We are the ones who must create the better world, a new world. And if that is how one thinks, then Christianity is dead (*30 Days*, Year XVI, Number 10, 1998, pp. 31-32).

HOW TO PREACH DOCTRINALLY

Here are seven guidelines for doctrinal preaching.

1. Doctrinal preaching must effectively incorporate Church doctrine. The *Catechism* states: " 'The believer's act [of faith] does not terminate in the propositions, but in the realities [which they express].' All the same, we do approach these realities with the help of formulations of the faith which permit us to express the faith and to hand it on, to celebrate it in community, to assimilate and live on it more and more" (170). Thus, from the standpoint of content, doctrinal preaching must embody the truth comprising the dogmatic formulations of Church teaching.

Cardinal Ratzinger cautions us about the potential perishability of faith. He writes:

> Do not presuppose the faith but propose it. . . . Faith is not maintained automatically. It is not a "finished business"

169

that we can simply take for granted. The life of faith has to be constantly renewed . . . The chief points of faith . . . are always the issues that affect us most profoundly. They must be the permanent center of preaching (*Gospel, Catechesis, Catechism*, San Francisco: Ignatius Press, 1997, pp. 23, 24).

To aid in this effort, it benefits the preacher to keep on hand reliable resources such as the NCCB/USCC *Preaching Guide*, or the *Our Sunday Visitor Encyclopedia of Catholic Doctrine*.

One crucial caution to keep in mind: Whereas doctrinal preaching incorporates the truth of the Church's dogmatic propositions in its *substance*, doctrinal preaching should not be propositional in its *presentation*.

2. The cardinal principle of doctrinal preaching is this: *People will live the Truth once they are led to love the Truth*. Thus, the objective of doctrinal preaching is to persuade people to use their free will to make decisions and choices in keeping with the teaching of the Church that imbue them with personal conviction and intellectual certitude. This conviction must be the fruit of critical thinking — not coercion, capitulation, or compromise.

Clearly, moralizing has no place in doctrinal preaching. The preacher has no right to tell people what to do without first clarifying why they should do it and how grace effects it. Doctrinal preaching must make explicit the gracious initiative of God, for the Gospel is the revelation in Jesus Christ of God's mercy to sinners. As Pope John Paul II explains, "Proclamation or kerygma is a call to conversion, announcing the truth of Christ, which reaches its summit in his Paschal Mystery; for only in Christ is it possible to know the fullness of the truth which saves" (*Fides et Ratio,* 99). Concrete, personal reference to Jesus Christ in the conception, formulation, and delivery of a homily preserves the preacher from the snares of moralism.

The Catechism emphasizes that "Christ did not live his life for himself but *for us*. . . . Christ enables us *to live in him* all that he himself lived, and *he lives it in us*" (519, 521). Von Balthasar corroborates this insight when he writes:

What is first of all clear is the dogmatic truth about the person and achievement of Christ and that one must proceed from it, and thus 'from above,' to deduce from this truth the rules of Christian life (*ibid.*, p. 63).

Therefore, as Cardinal Schönborn observes, whatever the Gospel calls us to do will always be a response to God and to his works *(ibid.,* p. 48). Accordingly, the onus is on the doctrinal preacher to represent the desirability of the Truth, who is Christ, in such a way that God's people elect to respond in a life of moral rectitude.

3. Doctrinal preaching must promote and demonstrate the reasonableness of the faith. One of the most compelling advocates of this nonnegotiable is Monsignor Luigi Guissani in his landmark book *The Religious Sense.* The Gospel is catholic: it is universal in its outreach; it is accessible and comprehendible to all. Thus, the claims of Christianity remain "rational" not simply to those who profess the Creed, but to any human being by virtue of his or her rationality. As Cardinal Schönborn insists:

Doctrine is not opposed to life. How can we love without understanding? Faith education must also be an education of the *intellectus fidei.* The understanding of faith deepens the trust in this faith and so the confidence in the way of life faith teaches us (*ibid.*, p. 57).

4. Doctrinal preaching must be communicated in an idiom that appeals to the current mentality. Communication is not what is said, but rather what is heard. Thus, doctrinal preaching must be "hearable." Much good preaching gets missed precisely because the preacher fails to translate his message into a engaging, timely vernacular. This dimension of doctrinal preaching is so vital that the Code of Canon Law asserts that "Christian doctrine is to be proposed in a manner accommodated to the condition of its listeners and adapted to the needs of the times" (Can. 769).

5. Doctrinal preaching must engage the imagination of the hearers. Doctrinal preaching is not teaching. While there is a catechetical aspect to it, doctrinal preaching can never be a surrogate for catechetics.

Preaching that restricts itself to the realm of the cognitive — to ideas — precludes a satisfying personal encounter with Jesus Christ. Preaching that is not "fascinating" in this respect is inferior. Doctrinal preaching must not deprive people of the stimulation that prompts them to form Gospel judgments and to come to their own Christian conclusions. That is the intended "entertaining" element of preaching.

Thus, to preach doctrinally is to preach like Jesus Christ. The incorporation of parables and parabolic structure remains key to authentic doctrinal preaching. For parable employs a strategic pattern of orientation, disorientation, and reorientation that engages both the intellect and the will of hearers, thereby stimulating their freedom to commit to the true, the good, and the beautiful with deliberate, self-invested resolve. In short, by interacting with imagination, doctrinal preaching offers the hearers a creative way to be obedient to the Gospel.

6. Gauge the soundness of doctrinal preaching by monitoring homiletic verb choice. Verbs like "strive," "should," and others that endemically eclipse God's initiative and that sidestep the agency of grace have little if any place in doctrinal preaching.

7. The aim of doctrinal preaching is reconciliation. Well executed doctrinal preaching will expunge all falsehood masquerading as truth. At the same time, doctrinal preaching reconciles apparently contradictory, confusing, inconvenient, irrelevant, unfashionable, or seemingly antiquated truths with the one Truth, Jesus Christ.

To sum it all up in the words of St. Paul, "As for yourself, you must say what is consistent with doctrine" (Ti 2:1). Then doctrinal preaching will be a gateway to contemplation and an instrument of freedom that preserves Mystery for the human mind while guaranteeing that our experience of the Mystery will be a personal and living one.

INDEX

Entires for such words as "Christ," "Church," "God," etc., that appear on almost every page of the text are listed with the first page on which the word occurs followed by *"et passim."*

175